W9-CIX-240

POINT OF THE LANCE

SARGENT SHRIVER:

18 17

POINT OF THE LANCE

HARPER & ROW, PUBLISHERS

NEW YORK, EVANSTON, AND LONDON

The chapter entitled "Who Is Responsible for the Poor?" originally appeared in *America—The National Catholic Weekly Review,* published by the Jesuit Fathers in New York.

The chapter entitled "Two Years of the Peace Corps" is adapted from an article written for *Foreign Affairs,* July 1963. Copyright © 1963 by Council on Foreign Relations, Inc., New York.

POINT OF THE LANCE. *Copyright © 1964 by Harper & Row, Publishers, Incorporated. Printed in the United States of America. For information address Harper & Row, Publishers, Incorporated, 49 East 33rd Street, New York 16, N. Y.*

Public speeches and documents in this book are in the public domain.

FIRST EDITION

LIBRARY OF CONGRESS CATALOG CARD NUMBER: 64-25288

K-O

To Eunice, the one most responsible for whatever merit is found in this book

Publisher's Note

Since the beginning of the Peace Corps, Harper & Row has looked forward to a book by Sargent Shriver. The first editor of Harper & Row to read a representative selection of Mr. Shriver's speeches was so impressed by the breadth of vision and experience embracing so much that is vital to America's world position that he proposed the publication of this book. With Mr. Shriver's permission, Harper & Row has edited and published this collection of talks and writings with the conviction that the ideas presented here will be of lasting interest at home and abroad.

To provide some of the history behind these ideas, and to apply the principles and experience of the Peace Corps to domestic and world affairs generally, Mr. Shriver, at the publisher's request, has written the new material in Part I, and supplied contextual and introductory material elsewhere as appropriate.

Contents

A SECTION OF ILLUSTRATIONS FOLLOWS PAGE 82

Acknowledgments

The "front lines" of the Peace Corps are overseas. The primary credit for our success, therefore, goes—with my deep appreciation—to the Volunteers abroad and to those men and women who have directed Peace Corps operations in each country. Our Peace Corps Country Representatives are listed in the Appendix. Their personal leadership in developing and guiding our programs is the least known but most vital factor in the overseas achievements. Without their management ability and qualities of personal leadership the Peace Corps would not have succeeded.

In Washington, an unusual group of dedicated Americans have labored with imagination and good judgment to support the overseas work. To all of them I express my special personal appreciation.

SARGENT SHRIVER

I

"THE SECRET OF YOUR GREATNESS"

"It is indeed striking that this important idea,
the most powerful idea in recent times, of a Peace
Corps . . . should come from this mightiest nation
on earth, the United States. Many of us who did not
know about the United States thought of this great
nation as a wealthy nation, a powerful nation,
endowed with great material strength and many
powerful weapons. But how many of us know that in
the United States ideas and ideals are also powerful?
This is the secret of your greatness."
—THANAT KHOMAN, Foreign Minister of Thailand,
Chulalongkorn University, Bangkok,
January 28, 1964

1. *Punta de Lanza*

"The peace corps is your *punta de lanza*—the point of your lance."

The revolutionary-minded Minister of National Economy in Bolivia who said this to me is serious about his military metaphors: in times past he is said to have put down his pistol on the table in front of him even during cabinet meetings. But Señor Gumucio also knows the power of an idea. He saw the Peace Corps as the human, cutting edge of the *Alianza para el Progreso*, as the sharpest thrust of the United States policy of supporting democratic change in Latin America. Our Volunteers, he said, were penetrating through all the barriers of protocol, bureaucracy, language, culture, and national frontiers to the people themselves. "They are reaching the minds and hearts of people."

The point of the lance is lean, hard, focused. It reaches its target. In our complex world that is what our political programs must do. And the "lance" Señor Gumucio referred to was a political one, with more than a Latin-American meaning. It represents the force of ideas and of people in action. Since "there is no alternative to peace," this is the most effective power we have.

It is unusual to view the Peace Corps in a political perspec-

5

tive. The Corps has become so nonpartisan at home and has always been so nonpolitical abroad that it is said to be the one major new program enjoying the simultaneous support of Hubert Humphrey and Barry Goldwater. The War on Poverty and our other domestic affairs do not directly concern world peace. But we can achieve peace in its full sense, at home and in the world, only if we understand the political nature of the problems before us and practice this new kind of politics of peace effectively, and on a world scale.

This position is supported by the experienced military strategists. They see that political factors take precedence today in most parts of the world. About the struggle in Vietnam, former Ambassador Henry Cabot Lodge, seconding General Bedell Smith, says that "any second-rate general could win in Indochina if there were a proper political atmosphere." T. E. Lawrence meant the same thing when he wrote of his desert revolt that "war upon rebellion was messy and slow, like eating soup with a knife." His Arabs did not advance with banners, he said; they became instead "an influence, an idea, a thing intangible, invulnerable, without front or back, drifting like a gas." The Arab revolution succeeded because "our kingdoms lay in each man's mind."

That is where our kingdoms used to be—in the days when American weapons were few and our economy underdeveloped, when we exercised boldly the power of our ideas and were an influence everywhere. Kingdoms are still to be found in men's minds.

Let me emphasize that the politics of ideas is not party politics. The problems are too large and too important to be left to normal political methods. That is one reason why military terminology is used in the Peace *Corps* and the *War* on Poverty. To eliminate poverty at home, and to achieve peace in the world, we need the total commitment, the large-scale mobilization, the institutional invention, the unprecedented release of human energy, and the focusing of intellect which have happened in our society only in war. We need what William James called "the moral equivalent of war."

The Peace Corps is just one example of the new politics of peace. In this age when the nuclear stalemate and the danger of total devastation limit the use of military power, we must rediscover and use what has always been our greatest power. The Foreign Minister of Thailand has spoken to us on this very point. "The secret of your greatness," he has advised the American people, "is the power of American ideas and ideals." It is a secret, however, which he believes we have not adequately shared with the world. "How many of us," he says on behalf of the people of Thailand, "know that in the United States ideas and ideals are powerful?"

It may be surprising to hear that few people in the rest of the world know that in the United States ideas and ideals are powerful. "Secret" power to us usually means some secret weapon. When we read of an "Invisible Government" we assume it means the CIA. But the people of the world find our weapons and our wealth most visible; and they see the operations of the CIA much more than any of us here at home. What is invisible or "secret" to them is what is most visible to us: the vitality of our democratic life—the great network of our private voluntary agencies, the work of community organizations from the PTA to the Red Cross, our labor unions, our service clubs, and our business enterprises, the whole force of our town, city, county, and state governments, and of federal programs such as TVA and Social Security; and our individual liberty, free speech, and free elections. This power that made America, the power of democratic action, has not yet been sufficiently seen by others or explained by us in other parts of the world.

This is not just a matter of American politics. Neither the Peace Corps nor the War on Poverty nor any of the talks and writings in this book is aimed primarily at any national American election. They are rather aimed at the world "election" now under way on every continent. The politics involved here is essentially the world politics in which we are all engaged.

For there is a continuous universal election going on in the world. Most of the constituencies do not have a two-party system or a secret ballot. Much of the voting takes place outside election booths. The "returns" are measured in terms of people fed, jobs found, schools built, children educated, bodies cured, economies growing, or in terms of fallen regimes, violent revolutions, hunger and despair. What is being decided is nothing less than the future of the human race.

The results of this fundamental decision-making process in the world community are seen in the councils of the United Nations, in summit meetings of statesmen, in the regional alliances of nations. But this is the surface. The source of any political process is the minds and hearts of people. It is in the towns and villages, on farms and in factories, in unions and in schools, wherever people live and work and talk and learn, that world politics begins. It is there, too, where revolutions and wars begin—and where peace begins.

Today we see the beginnings of peace even in the midst of military crises. War is the extension of politics by other means, said a German military strategist. But war is the breakdown of politics. Peace is the result of justice and law, which can come only through a working international political process. The prospects for peace improve as this process becomes more powerful. We can help this process by seeing and seizing all the new opportunities now opening. For the world is no longer divided into just two armed camps: Soviet Communism and the West. There are important political divisions within each of these camps, and even greater divisions cutting across the world: the north-south division between the economically developed northern countries and the newly developing southern continents; and the racial division between the white minority and the colored majority of the human race.

General Marshall saw this coming fifteen years ago. "We are in the middle of the world revolution—and I don't mean Communism," he said at Honolulu after a trip to Asia. "The Communists are like your surf riders here; they're just moving in on the crest of a wave. The revolution I'm talking about is that of the little people all over the world. They're beginning to learn what there is in life, and to learn what they are missing."

That is the revolution of which the Peace Corps and the War on Poverty are part. Fortunately, the course of this revolution is still largely peaceful. Our purpose is to keep it peaceful and moving in freedom. In this process of constructive world politics Peace Corps Volunteers are some of our first "precinct workers."

The problems are complex; their resolution is difficult. But by listening to, and working with, and understanding the people of the world—by being political in the best sense—we have the unprecedented opportunity to devise and carry out a successful strategy of peace.

2. A Creative Hour for Ideas

Harper & Row asked Sargent Shriver to describe the early days of the Peace Corps and the War on Poverty.

JOHN KENNEDY first proposed the Peace Corps in Ann Arbor, Michigan, at about 2 A.M. on October 14, 1960. Arriving late and finding a large crowd of students and faculty still waiting, he presented the idea as a question. Speaking extemporaneously, with no one carefully recording his remarks, he asked if they were ready to work in Asia, Africa, and Latin America, living on a modest scale, giving a part of their lives to such service. He asked what they would think if a new administration undertook to organize a Peace Corps to make this possible.

Then and in the weeks to follow, the response was remarkable. At Toledo, Ohio, some days later, a delegation of Michigan students came with a petition signed by several hundred who said they were ready. Stimulated by this response, John Kennedy proposed the Peace Corps in a major address at the Cow Palace in San Francisco on November 2, 1960.

No one is sure just why Kennedy raised the question in the middle of the night at the University of Michigan. Perhaps someone told him that at Michigan there was an active campus committee called "Americans Committed to World Responsibility" championing the idea. The idea certainly was in the air. Versions of it called a "Youth Corps" or a "National Service Corps" were before Congress, in bills by Senator Hubert Humphrey, Representative Henry Reuss, and others. General James Gavin and others had proposed something like it to Kennedy. Probably similar proposals were made to Richard Nixon. But it was still "just an idea."

It might still be just an idea but for the affirmative response of those Michigan students and faculty. Possibly Kennedy would have tried it once more on some other occasion, but without a strong popular response he would have concluded the idea was impractical or premature. That probably would have ended it then and there. Instead, it was almost a case of spontaneous combustion.

Some are amazed that what was "only a campaign idea" has become an established American institution. The truth is that the Peace Corps owes much of its success to its birth in a political campaign. A national Presidential campaign is, in a way, close to a kind of war—a war carried on in peaceful, political ways. The Peace Corps started out with, and has tried to keep, the momentum and unbureaucratic spontaneity of the 1960 campaign.

But American history is full of unfulfilled campaign promises. In this case the gap between promise and fulfillment became a creative "spark-gap." After the election, while some of us were conducting a "talent hunt" to help the President-elect find the key men to serve the new administration, we received more letters from people offering to work in, or to volunteer for, the Peace Corps, which did not then exist, than for all existing agencies in the United States Government put together. Over thirty thousand Americans wrote to support the idea.

Because of this response of the American people President Kennedy decided to establish the Peace Corps as one of his first major acts. This is an example of what Martin Buber calls "the meeting of idea and fate in a creative hour." It is the way ideas are born in American politics.

President Kennedy picked me to organize the Peace Corps, I was told, because no one thought the Peace Corps could succeed and it would be easier to fire a relative than a political friend.

Perhaps he asked me to undertake this assignment because he considered it not unlike those he had given me during and after the campaign. In July, 1960, he had asked me to organize several campaign groups concerned with major issues. This was a new approach, emphasizing his interest in ideas. Instead of campaign sections for the "Negro vote" or the "farmer's vote" or the vote of the city people, we organized sections on civil rights, on farm problems, and on urban affairs. Our task was to bring together the key leaders in these fields, to advise the candidates on the issues, and to begin planning what a new administration should do. This deepened the commitment to some important campaign promises. It also contributed to the Kennedy-Johnson ticket's success in securing the vote of people deeply concerned.

A few days after the new administration took office, with the remaining recommendations of our postelection talent hunt turned over to the newly appointed cabinet officers, the President asked me to report to him how the Peace Corps could be organized and then to organize it. I agreed to do the report but, despite deep interest in the idea, urged him to select someone else as director of the organization.

My interest in direct American participation in the development of other nations started in the 1930's when I was a part of, and later a leader for, Experiment in International Living groups in Europe. After visits to several Asian countries in the 1950's, including Japan, Korea, Vietnam, Cambodia, and Thailand, I proposed a plan of sending three-man political action teams to Asia, Africa, and Latin America. These teams were to consist of vigorous and imaginative young labor leaders, businessmen, and politicians. They would offer their services at a grass-roots level and work directly with the people, contributing to the growth of the economies, to the democratic organization of the societies, and to the peaceful outcome of the social revolutions under way. The Peace Corps offered the possibility of realizing, in a new form, this old idea.

I resisted the assignment at first and proposed other people because I wished to protect the President from additional charges of nepotism and to enable the Peace Corps to start with the fewest possible disadvantages. It had already been dubbed "Kennedy's Kiddie Korps" by some. Mr. Nixon said the Corps would be a "haven for draft dodgers." Former President Eisenhower called it a "juvenile experiment." Others ridiculed it as a "children's crusade."

President Kennedy wanted to make it tough and effective, and prove the skeptics wrong. A man of few words, he ignored my doubts, and just said, "Go ahead. You can do it."

To "do it" we assembled the best people we could find from the professional worlds, from our universities and great foundations, from our corporations and unions, from private agencies and the Civil Service. Their experience was all pertinent, because the Peace Corps had unusual management problems, and was to be a vast new educational enterprise. "I use not only all the brains I have, but all I can borrow," Woodrow Wilson said. So did we. We knew the Peace Corps would have only one chance to work. As with the parachute jumper, the chute had to open the first time.

The President's task force on a Peace Corps worked literally day and night for weeks. It was like the hectic, hard-pressed period of the campaign. We knew that speed was essential in order not to lose the momentum of the idea among the people who were asking, "What *can* we do for our country?"

By March 1, 1961, we were ready with a detailed report to the President which recommended the Peace Corps' immediate establishment. "No matter how well conceived and efficiently run, there probably will be failures," our report warned. "These could be costly and have a serious effect both at home and abroad." But we placed our faith in its promise, and stated what in effect became the three purposes of the Peace Corps later adopted by Congress:

It can contribute to the development of critical countries and regions. It can promote international cooperation and goodwill toward this country. It can also contribute to the education of America and to more intelligent American participation in the world.

We put special stress on what the Peace Corps could do for this country. "It is time for American universities to become truly world universities," our report said. By involving universities on a large scale, thus expanding their teaching and research to the world, the Peace Corps would "help with this transformation." The report concluded: "All this may combine to provide a substantial popular base for responsible American policies toward the world. And this is meeting the world's need, too, since what the world most needs from this country is better understanding of the world."

Within a few days, the President established the Peace Corps by Executive Order, while requesting permanent legislation from Congress. He encouraged me to accept invitations to visit a number of countries which had already asked to talk about the Peace Corps. The first invitations came from Prime Minister Nehru and President Ayub Khan. Other invitations rapidly followed, and as a consequence, during May, 1961, I visited the heads of state and prime ministers in Ghana, Nigeria, Pakistan, India, Burma, Malaya, Thailand, and the Philippines. All of them expressed interest and support and emphasized the need they had for just the kind of "middle-level" manpower we hoped to provide. This was the missing link in their development plans: men and women willing and able to do the skilled work of schoolteaching, community action, agricultural extension, and public health until local people could be trained to do all this themselves.

While I was traveling to these countries, a critical event occurred at home. Without it, the Peace Corps would not be where it is today.

Vice President Johnson had agreed to serve as chairman of the Peace Corps' National Advisory Committee. In that capacity, he learned from me, just as I was leaving for Africa, that the President's advisers on foreign aid programs had decided against our recommendation that the Peace Corps be established as an autonomous agency. Lyndon Johnson saw the need politically, in Congress, in the country, and in the world, for the Peace Corps to have a special identity. He went to President Kennedy and persuaded him to give the Peace Corps a life of its own.

In a very real sense Lyndon Johnson is a founding father of the Peace Corps. The organizational charts would have looked better if we had become a box in a single foreign aid agency. But the thrust of a new idea would have been lost. The new wine needed a new bottle.

So the creation of the Peace Corps was not spontaneous. It took men of politics like Kennedy and Johnson who could invent an institution to embody a new idea. And it needed men and women in the Peace Corps administration in Washington with a spirit like that of the Volunteers we were sending abroad. Our staff and Volunteers would have to come from both parties and from the even larger American party, the party of nonparty people.

They would be Volunteers representing that quality in American life which de Tocqueville more than a century ago saw as the central source of American strength. It is a quality we needed to tap anew. It is part of our political power we needed to apply to the world.

This was the idea we put at the heart of the Peace Corps' first presentation to Congress. On June 22, 1961, I began our testimony to the Senate Foreign Relations Committee with a question:

One month ago in India, Ashadevi, an extraordinary woman and former associate of the late Mahatma Gandhi, traveled three days and nights on a train to come to New Delhi to talk with me about the Peace Corps.

"Yours was the first revolution," she said. "Do you think young Americans possess the spiritual values they must have to bring the spirit of that revolution to our country?

"There is a great valuelessness spreading around the world and in India, too," she said. "Your Peace Corps Volunteers must bring more than science and technology. They must touch the idealism of America and bring that to us, too. Can they do it?"

That was the question: "Can we do it?" Our answer, based on faith, was "Yes."

While Congress was considering the new Act, the first training program for Volunteers had begun, and in September, when the Act was passed, the first groups of Volunteers were already overseas, in Ghana, Tanganyika, Colombia, Chile, and the Philippines.

The "juvenile experiment" had begun. We felt confident it would work, but we remembered the proverb we had heard in Africa: "Until you have crossed the river, don't insult the crocodile's mouth."

Today the situation is different. With twelve thousand American men and women, of all ages, having served in the Peace Corps in forty-six countries, with the first three thousand Volunteers home after two years of successful work, with practically all these countries and a dozen others on the "waiting list" asking for more Volunteers, with over 100,000 Americans having applied to serve, we have passed the first crocodiles. But we are still "crossing the river."

To keep the Peace Corps alive and alert, we look forward to returning Volunteers taking over its administration. To promote this, we have had from the beginning an unusual government policy known as "in—up—and out." We are proposing a limit of five years on the staff for any one employee, including the director. In a few years we expect the Peace Corps to be manned largely by those who have had overseas experience in its service.

Knowing these Volunteers, I am confident they will keep the Peace Corps true to its unfolding mission. Their spirit was expressed by one of the first two Volunteers to lose their lives, in an air accident while serving in Colombia. Writing to his parents, David Crozier said: "Should it come to it, I had rather give my life trying to help someone than to have to give my life looking down a gun barrel at them."

The War on Poverty is being organized in much the same way as the Peace Corps. We know what President Johnson wants us to do: to proceed with the same sense of urgency, to gather the same kind of momentum, to tap the same volunteer spirit, to take the same basic approach to people and their problems at home as the Peace Corps has done overseas. To invent the new institutions needed to combat poverty at home, we have again called together a task force of people from labor and business, from education and welfare work, from federal agencies, and from local action programs across the country. And again, because this is a time when ideas and talent are welcome in Washington, outstanding men and women have responded and helped.

We are seeking to create a genuine partnership for constructive action—the broadest and most effective partnership of city, state and federal governments and of the people working together that this nation has ever seen. When Lyndon Johnson says, "Come, let us reason together," he means, "Come, let us work together."

Like the Peace Corps, the Economic Opportunity Program (as we prefer to call the War on Poverty) will be entirely voluntary. No one will enter the Job Corps or serve as a Volunteer in the program unless he asks to; no community will receive assistance for its community action program unless it asks for it.

Like the Peace Corps, the focus is on young people and their education. Education is the way to break the vicious circle that continues poverty from generation to generation.

The Job Corps, for example, goes straight to this educational target. It will penetrate to the streets of every slum in this nation: to the young men and women caught in the hard core of poverty. It will offer them two years of hard work and good education in an entirely new environment, where for the first time they will be given a full opportunity to develop as productive citizens.

Some of the Job Corps centers will do conservation work on our public lands and in state forests and parks. These will resemble the CCC camps of Franklin Roosevelt's days with the important addition of special educational and training opportunities. Even more important will be the Job Corps' residential education centers. These will be different from anything that has existed in American education before. Perhaps they should be called public boarding schools—where special education will be offered those most in need of it. In these communities of work and study, we will try to bring together all the new techniques of teaching and provide the best possible curriculum, teachers, teaching aids, counselors, job experience, and living conditions.

The Job Corps and the other youth education and work opportunities in the President's program—particularly in the local community action programs—are thus one answer to the hopelessness of the young men and women taking out their frustration in violence.

Part of the answer to violence in our streets is action to restrain those inciting it or engaging in it—action *against* all extremists, whether black nationalists or white nationalists, whether Communist or Ku Klux Klan. But action *for* new economic opportunities is a larger part of the answer. Putting on the lid is clearly not enough. This nation's proper response to what has been happening in many areas of racial strife is effective action to end the poverty that breeds violence.

Fortunately, a national consensus in support of this program is emerging. Many Republican legislators voted their consciences in supporting the Economic Opportunity Act. And much honor is due the Southern legislators who were subjected to malicious political attacks stressing that the bill would help Negroes. Aroused by the attempt to embarass him with his white constituents in Georgia, Congressman Phil Landrum, co-author of the bill, made this statement:

I want it clearly understood . . . that any assistance that it may provide toward eliminating the blight of poverty affecting Americans of all races is a source of pride to me. I am not ashamed of it. I come from a section of the country that has been bombarded with a great deal of demagoguery. There are many, many Negroes in all sections of the country who are poor. There are many, many white people in all sections of the country who are poor. I want it clearly understood that my efforts . . . are directed toward relieving poverty that affects both white and Negro Americans.

The War on Poverty, like the Peace Corps, goes beyond any party, any President—and certainly beyond any administrator. It can hurt no one. It can help everyone. It can reach to the people who have been left out or left behind. It can bring them into the mainstream of American life. When the power of these millions of bypassed Americans is released, all of America will be stronger, richer, and more secure.

3. The Party of Hope

THERE HAVE BEEN TWO PARTIES throughout history, Emerson
said: the Party of Memory and the Party of Hope. Jefferson put
it another way: "Men are naturally divided into two parties.
Those who fear and distrust the people . . . and those who identify themselves with the people."

In an increasingly complex world these generalizations may
appear too simple. But the divisions seen by Emerson and
Jefferson are still the battle lines. "The Party of Conservatism
and that of Innovation are very old," as Emerson wrote in
1841. "It is the opposition of Past and Future."

What is new is the world-wide scope of these political
divisions. What is at stake is not just the outcome of a national
election or the course of a national administration; what is at
stake is the fate of the human race. "We are all of us," wrote
the author of *Richer by Asia*, "consciously or unconsciously,
waking or sleeping, building the unity of man or plotting the
end of the world."

In framing our programs and policies we must ask whether
they contribute to the Party of Hope in the world, whether
they promote democratic innovation and peaceful change,
whether they build the unity of man. To do this we must

understand the variety of forces shaping our own and the world's political process. Looking at five major arenas of world political struggle—the arenas of religion, of world Communism, of the newly developing nations, of the American civil rights struggle, and of American party politics—we see the age-old "opposition of Past and Future."

It may seem strange to consider the Catholic Church under the category of politics. Stalin asked scornfully: How many battalions has the Pope? But for twenty centuries the Catholic Church has been one of the main carriers of our Western civilization. The course of Church policy, in fact, involves a most profound politics, affecting all religions and nations, and world peace itself.

Never have the two parties, of Memory and Hope, contended more vigorously or openly than in the Vatican Councils called by Pope John and continued by Pope Paul. The men considering Church policy divide naturally into two parties, those who fear and distrust a breakdown of hierarchy and a transfer of power from the Curia and the Congregations in Rome to the bishops, priests, and laymen—and those who wish the Church to identify itself with the people of the world, of all colors, of all creeds, on all continents.

John XXIII's call for an *aggiornamento*, an opening up and bringing up to date of the Church, struck the new note. For too long the bells of the Church had seemed to ring in memory of the past, of saints long dead, of a ritual in an alien and dead language, of a conservative tradition.

With new realism and urgency the Church is facing the problems of the world: racial justice, national independence, religious liberty, economic justice, population planning, world peace. The ideas were all there, deep within the Church, and expressed by some of the Church's greatest thinkers. But the lid had to be taken off, so that these fundamental principles could be applied to the present day. With Paul VI, the work of modernization goes on, with new impetus to its central focus: the Ecumenical movement.

There are those in the Church who oppose the new Office for Christian Unity, who look askance when the Pope meets with leaders of the Anglican and Protestant churches, with leaders of the American Jewish Committee, even with Mr. Khrushchev's son-in-law. The "Party of Memory" has resisted the Church's condemnation of prejudice toward Jews, and its recognition of the right to religious liberty everywhere, for Protestants and others in Catholic countries as much as for Catholics in countries where they are a minority. This party of the past does not understand the need to make the world safe for diversity.

The difficulties are not easily resolved. Overpopulation and the problem of family planning must be faced. The "wide and profound . . . grave and honest" review of this question now under way in the Church is needed. Modern answers can be found that will respect the holy mission of marriage, enhance love, and enable men to control the population explosion morally and rationally, if the best minds turn to science in hope and not in fear.

Not the least of the new attributes of the *aggiornamento* is the good humor and relaxation of old tensions emanating from Vatican City. When John was asked how many people work in the Vatican, he replied: "About half." In Jerusalem last January those of us who witnessed the meeting of Pope Paul and the Patriarch Athenagoras realized that these men belong to the Party of Hope.

Fortunately, a relaxation of tensions and opening to the future is not a phenomenon limited to the Vatican. There are signs of it in the other great world forces, even within the Communist empire.

Mr. Khrushchev swings like a pendulum from shoe-beating in the UN to baby-kissing in Scandinavia, but his de-Stalinization program is a profound fact in the Soviet-ruled part of the world. The party of Memory—the old "dogmatists," in Communist jargon—is weaker in Russia, now that Khrushchev has let the Russian people know the inside horrors of Stalin's rule. In Eastern Europe, where Russian domination has been so suffocating, the people have necessarily looked to the future for hope; in tentative innovation some of them have reached a measure of national autonomy.

Although the fanaticism of the Chinese Communists makes the Kremlin appear to be mild "revisionists" by comparison, it is not Khrushchev who represents the Party of Hope. In the Soviet bloc, it is the younger generation, men like the young poet Yevtushenko, who dream of a transformed, more humane Communism. We should not forget that the vanguard of the Hungarian Revolution and of the upheaval in Poland were young Communists who rose against the frustration of their dream.

In China we see few signs of this ferment. But we cannot get passports to China. It is clear, however, that the whole Communist world is in a process of division and change. No one can predict whether the thaw will continue or whether those who fear the people will again turn back the season in Eastern Europe or even crush the growing independence in the arts in Russia. But the existence of the two parties, deep within Soviet society, is clear.

In Africa, Asia, and Latin America, those natural political divisions are clear and present, too. Sometimes they meet in one man's mind. In discussions of world affairs with Presidents Nkrumah, Sekou Touré, and Sukarno, I have felt their bitter memories of the Western colonialism they suffered so long, and at the same time their hopeful response to the Peace Corps and to some other American policies.

At the heads of state meeting in Addis Ababa, there were two approaches taken. Ethiopia's Emperor Haile Selassie, Tanganyika's President Julius Nyerere, Nigeria's Prime Minister Sir Abubakar Balewa, and others called on Africa to forget past injustices and focus on present problems and the possible vast future. In contrast were those who spent their time denouncing Western imperialism.

Two poles of Memory and Hope are found within America. In the civil rights movement there are many capable leaders who have never lost their faith in people, including white people. Fortunately, there are millions of Negro Americans who have worked in this hope, despite all disappointment. But there are also many angry men, embittered by discrimination, who in the name of black nationalism or by resort to violence and disorder have turned their backs on all white people and all democratic progress.

Both of our great political parties are divided along these ancient lines, with extremists such as those in the John Birch Society and the Ku Klux Klan unhappily on the fringes of both parties. Yet the pendulum of our politics has rarely swung to the extremes. The Party of Hope carries the country forward, whether its political instrument is the Democratic-Republican Party of Thomas Jefferson, or the Democratic Party of Andrew Jackson, or the Republican Party of Abraham Lincoln and Theodore Roosevelt. The Party of Memory holds us back, whether with the Democratic Party of James Buchanan or the Republican Party of Warren G. Harding. As Emerson wrote, "First the one, then the other holds the day, and then the struggle begins anew."

In recent years, the Party of Hope and Innovation has prevailed, first with John Kennedy, now with Lyndon Johnson. Both men have understood what the geopoliticians tend to forget: that along with territory, material resources, and weapons, power has another vital element, the element which created the American Revolution and which is carrying on all the revolutions of our time. This is the power of the people— even the poor, the ignorant, the hungry people. The central problem of American world policy is to use this power of the people intelligently and effectively. And for this, we must know and identify ourselves with the hopes and aspirations of the world's people.

The success of Kennedy and Johnson comes from their being men of politics. They have had faith in people and an identification with people. And this gave them a sense of political reality that would tell them not to think or talk in terms of nuclear defoliation, or of a return to normalcy. Instead, they have spoken of the American revolution "intended for all mankind," of "man's vast future," of a New Freedom, a New Deal, and a Great Society. And they have been innovators.

But we must be not just followers of great men but builders of a Great Society. The test of leadership is the response of the people. The primary problem in the world is releasing the power of people to effect change, to make reforms, to carry through social revolutions peacefully, to build new nations, to create a peaceful world society.

Only in this way can we help the forces of peace and constructive change at home and in the world; only in this way can we assure victory for the Party of Hope, not on any one election day, not in any one nation, but in our time and on all continents.

The following suggestions are directed to the problem of releasing the power of the world's people and harnessing it in democratic action.

WITH THE NEWLY-DEVELOPING NATIONS OF ASIA, AFRICA, AND LATIN AMERICA, we must be clear about our aim. What we are seeking is not the support of these nations but their success. If they succeed in their plans for economic, social, and political progress, it will not matter much whether they agree or disagree with us, even whether they like us. If they become healthy democratic societies in their own right, they will not become threats to world peace.

Our military assistance necessarily goes to those places under

Communist attack or in danger of armed subversion or aggression. Our political and economic assistance should on the other hand give special attention to those places where a peaceful outcome is still possible. Most of the continent of Africa meets this test. So does the India-Pakistan subcontinent where half of the people of the developing nations live. So does most of Latin America. We must not let the inevitable military preoccupation with Vietnam, Cuba, Korea, the Congo, and with China and Russia prevent us from seeing and acting upon the great waiting opportunities in the rest of the world.

The time to act politically is before violent revolution or war stirs us to last-minute military action. Then we would start pouring in billions of dollars of military aid, and even our own men and arms if necessary. Is it beyond our capacity to act creatively ahead of such a crisis?

In the Peace Corps we have shown that effective and creative action is possible. Every Peace Corps Volunteer is advancing freedom and peace. For if he is serving as a schoolteacher, he is teaching the next generation how to think for themselves. If he is a community development worker, he is teaching people how to organize peacefully for themselves. If he is a doctor or a nurse, he is demonstrating the respect for every human being that is the first principle of freedom and peace.

Peace Corps Volunteers work in forty-six countries which are not on the front lines of the cold war. Yet the "Peace Corps" countries contain over one billion people. If we establish good relationships with these people, if we work with the effective forces of innovation among these people, if these nations join the "Party of Hope" in the world, then our future in world politics and all the world's prospects for peace will be bright.

There are some specific steps we can take:

We can double the size of the Peace Corps. Every country where the Peace Corps is operating is asking for more Volunteers, often for two, three, four times as many Volunteers. The needs are real in these and other countries requesting Volunteers. The opportunities exist. By providing many more Volunteers we can help these new nations move faster, we can help release the power of these people on a much greater scale. The ten-thousand-strong Peace Corps should now be doubled, so that at least twenty thousand Americans can serve overseas in this effective new grass-roots way.

Some of the Peace Corps lessons should be applied to our other overseas operations. More Americans serving abroad can live simply among the people with whom they are working. They can learn the local language; they can live on the local economy, without cheap, subsidized liquor and imported, duty-free luxury goods; they can give extra time in voluntary community service; they can make friends and give an example of democratic life outside "diplomatic ghettos"; they can be sensitive to local customs; they can understand and respect the ideas and aspirations of other people. Policies, incentives, and disciplines can and should be adopted by each of our overseas services to ensure this.

We can find more effective men to represent us abroad. Some of our great ambassadors in recent times have come out of American education, business, and labor, and from American politics—as well as from our career Foreign Service. Since diplomacy in two-thirds of the world has shifted to this more fundamental process of nation-building, it is not surprising that men who have succeeded in building organizations and working with people at home do well abroad. More men like this should be brought into our overseas service. To fill positions of high responsibility, a continuing Presidential "talent hunt" should seek out the best men from within and outside government.

We can invite other countries to send teachers and young leaders to America: a "reverse Peace Corps." Peace Corps Volunteers have discovered that what other peoples want most is not just our money, but our friendship and respect. Nothing would convey this better, both symbolically and practically, than our inviting other nations to select and send some of their teachers here for a year or two, not to study but to teach in our schools and serve in our community education programs. They can teach the history, culture, language, and art of their country or region. North Americans would be learning from Latin Americans. Asians and Africans would be teaching about the oldest and newest civilizations. Skilled Israeli youth workers, already successful in giving new hope and skills to demoralized young men and women, would give us "technical assistance."

This might release more of our teachers for work and study abroad. Through such a program the coming generation of Americans can learn firsthand about the other cultures and peoples of the world. The foreign participants can not only see a new dynamic side of America, but through their experience can learn new ways to solve their nations' problems. We can begin by inviting one thousand such teachers from abroad.

We can help other nations form their own Peace Corps. In 1962 an International Secretariat for Volunteer Services was established at an international conference arranged by the United States Peace Corps and presided over by Lyndon Johnson. Some forty nations are cooperating in this program to promote the organization of Peace Corps-type operations in other countries. Eight European nations now are sending Volunteers overseas and more than a dozen developing nations have started domestic national service movements within their own borders. As this world-wide volunteering movement grows, American Volunteers will find themselves working alongside volunteers from their host countries and volunteers from Europe, Great Britain, and Japan.

WITH THE NATIONS UNDER COMMUNISM, we can use the power of our philosophical, political, and cultural ideas to promote peaceful change within the Communist empire. With the ultimate aim of freedom for all peoples suffering under Communism, we should take every opportunity to reduce international tensions, to establish new people-to-people relations with the Communist world, and to negotiate whatever constructive government-to-government agreements are possible.

As Cardinal Wyszynski of Poland has stressed, the condition for freedom in Eastern Europe is peace. In periods of relative peace, the Kremlin and local Communist rulers have relaxed their grip in Eastern Europe.

No one can predict how far Soviet society can be transformed from within. No one can say how much American policy can do to affect the process. But we should keep alert to every opportunity and be, as President Johnson has said, "unceasing" and "resourceful in our pursuit of areas of agreement," and both "ready to defend the national interest and to negotiate the common interest."

Specifically, we can seek to extend the areas of practical cooperation into new fields such as outer space, the uses of the sea, and research on cancer and other medical problems. The small beginnings made in the treaty for international control and development of Antarctica, in the treaty banning nuclear tests aboveground, and with the direct line between the White House and the Kremlin, can be carried forward in other useful directions. The sea itself and the resources in and under the sea are a great new frontier for exploration and development. Desalinization through the use of nuclear energy may open vast new possibilities for irrigation of arid lands, and "sea farming" may provide new food for man's growing population. And international cooperation in medical research can assist significantly in the efforts to find the cure for our major diseases.

We can work to bring about a large-scale exchange of students and of people generally. It is clear that the movement of peoples is one of the keys to human understanding and peace. A great organized summer exchange of people is now under way between France and Germany. They are exchanging a quarter of a million students this summer alone. If these two ancient enemies can exchange a quarter of a million students in one season it should be feasible to work out annual exchange visits between ten thousand young people from Eastern Europe and the Soviet Union and ten thousand Americans. There will be great difficulties in arranging this, but if we press for it skillfully, not seeking to pile up debating points in the cold war but seeking agreement, the doors may be cautiously opened. This would give great encouragement to the people of Poland, Hungary, Czechoslovakia, Rumania, and Bulgaria, and to the Russian people who have been sealed off from the rest of the world. The small-scale cultural exchange agreements now in operation are a first hesitant step. But we must open our doors with much more confidence. We know our society can stand close scrutiny. We trust our people. Let us show the strength of our convictions by proposing a free movement of citizens unparalleled in history.

These steps are of merit in themselves. They can also contribute to the climate of peace which the Cardinal of Poland says is the precondition for freedom.

THE GREAT RELIGIONS OF THE WORLD are among the greatest forces for peace in the world. On occasion, religious militancy has brought on wars. Religion clearly plays a central part in the creation of a civilization. To create a true world community, the power of the great religions must be mobilized. Their leaders must join with the statesmen of the world to create the conditions of peace.

The World Council of Churches and the Ecumenical Council are beginning to do this within Christendom. The President of the United States should have representatives working with both those bodies and the churches they speak for. But a wider dialogue must be started, to include spokesmen for Judaism, Islam, Hinduism, and Buddhism, to name four other great religions. It must be focused on the problems of peace and world development, seeking new ways to release and apply the spiritual power of people to the solution of these problems. We must find Americans informed about these other religions who will help us promote this practical dialogue.

THE UNITED NATIONS is the central organ of the world community. We must, as President Kennedy pledged in his Inaugural Address, "enlarge the area where its writ may run." We must seek to develop it into a genuine world security system. From the relatively successful emergency "peace forces" in the Middle East, we should go on to create permanent United Nations "peace forces" ready for duty whenever and wherever necessary. We should also do everything possible to bring about effective arms control and arms reduction. But here, too, we should not develop the military side alone. The opportunities for growth of the social and economic work of the United Nations and its subsidiary agencies are limited only by the support given. Through these bodies and new institutions formed to deal with the new frontiers of the sea and of outer space and the peaceful uses of atomic energy, we can make a reality of the UN's "Decade of Development."

WITHIN THE UNITED STATES we must, as Lyndon Johnson said to Congress, "match national strength with national restraint."

The responsible role of a national administration in an age of mass communication is to focus the nation's attention and to mobilize its spiritual, human, and material resources for action on the great issues facing us. People everywhere can be inspired and encouraged to eradicate poverty in all corners of our life; to secure equal opportunity for all Americans; to ex-

pand our educational system; to provide medical care for the
aged and for all those in need; to carry out the automation of
our industries so as to promote the general welfare and protect
the interest of workers and of the particular enterprise; and to
carry on our Food for Peace program so as to put our agricultural abundance at the service of a still hungry world.

On all these fronts we have made beginnings. The complexity
of the problems is too much for some who cling to the memory
of a simpler time. But this generation of Americans *has* been
tempered by war and disciplined by a hard peace. Born in this
century, it sees the complexity as the very nature of the challenge. It responds, as Americans in all their greatest periods
have responded, to the voice of hope. To the urgency required,
this generation also adds patience. "Peace is a process," said
John Kennedy. "Peace is a journey," says Lyndon Johnson,
"a journey of a thousand miles, and it must be taken one step
at a time."

II

OUR

UNFINISHED

REVOLUTION

"The American Revolution has gone thundering on.
Nothing can stop it, not even the American hands that
first set it rolling."
— ARNOLD TOYNBEE

With the death of President Kennedy, the world wondered,
we all wondered, what America would do next. With the first
words of President Johnson, "I will do my best. I ask for your
help and God's," we began to know the answer.

As the new President stepped forward in the funeral proces-
sion, taking his place among the leaders of the world, as he
stood before Congress saying, "It is a time for action," people
saw America's strength. The talks in Part II explore the nature
of this strength, finding it in the fundamental ideas of the
American Revolution.

The American Revolution, now in strange forms and shapes
and going by other names, is rolling along among the world's
people. But "the leadership," as the British historian Toynbee
warns us, "has fallen into other hands."

To recapture that leadership and assure that the basic ideas
of our revolution are neither misunderstood nor misused, we
must continue our own "unfinished revolution" at home and
explain it and extend it abroad. The Peace Corps is just one example of how the American government and people can do this.

1. The First World-Wide Mourning

In January 1964, as Special Representative of President John-
son, Sargent Shriver delivered messages from the President to
Pope Paul VI, to the Patriarch of Constantinople, and to the
heads of state of Israel, Jordan, Turkey, Iran, Afghanistan,
Pakistan, India, Nepal, and Thailand. He visited Peace Corps
Volunteers in seven of these countries. Upon his return, he
gave the following speech to the National Press Club in
Washington on February 21, 1964.

Two POWERFUL IMPRESSIONS remain in my mind since my
recent trip around the world. First was the enormous impact of
President Kennedy's death on the people of the small towns
and villages of the entire world of free men. Second was the
impact the Peace Corps has had.

When I arrived in Israel, on the first leg of my trip, former
Prime Minister David Ben-Gurion told me that the death of
President Kennedy was the occasion of the "first world-wide
mourning in the history of man."

Our Volunteers in small Turkish villages told me how their
students had come to class after the assassination weeping
openly. In the countryside of Iran, one of our workers was
approached on November 22 by a fellow worker who, with

tears in his eyes, announced, *"Our* President is dead." In other towns of the Near and Far East people spontaneously assumed the garb of mourning. In several places local high schools searched for a flag, which they ordinarily did not use, just so they could fly it at half-mast. Everywhere, mayors and tribal chiefs, as well as kings and presidents, told us they had never seen such a universal outpouring of emotion, of grief and loss, at the death of a foreign leader.

I could multiply such stories a hundredfold. And I think it is typical of America that, as much as we admired President Kennedy, few in this country had any real conception of the place this man had found in the hearts and the hopes of the world's people.

Why was this so? What were the qualities of John F. Kennedy that he could reach into the villages of Turkey, penetrate the mud huts of the altiplano of Peru, become meaningful to illiterate workers in Nepal whose only contact with the outside world is a transistor radio? This is an important question because in the answer we will find a clearer understanding of our strength as a nation and of how we can use that strength to help create the kind of world we want.

Through the Peace Corps, I believe, we can find part of that answer. For the Peace Corps was his creation. In a unique way it reflected his ideas and qualities. And, consequently, it has had, in its own way, a similar impact among the people of the world.

In the Philippines the Peace Corps recently became the first non-Asian group to win the Ramón Magsaysay Award, given to persons in Asia who "exemplify in spirit, integrity and devotion to liberty" the late President of the Philippines.

In Arequipa, Peru, when the Peace Corps was attacked by local Communists, the answer came not from the government or diplomats, but from the "Asociación Urbana del Población Arequipeña," the slum dwellers of Arequipa, who live in some

of the worst conditions in the world. Their alcalde—or mayor
—said, "We raise our most energetic protest against the attitude
of a few persons who have not seen the reality of the benefits
being received by thousands of workers."

In the Dominican Republic a group of people were writing
"Yankee Go Home" on a wall, while one of our Volunteers
watched. When they finished he said, "I guess that means I'll
have to go home." They turned and said, "No, we mean Yankees,
not the Peace Corps."

The point was eloquently expressed by a local official in Sarawak, who said of the Volunteers who were helping him cut a
road through the jungle, "They're not your people any more;
they're mine."

This point was made to President Kennedy. "Do you know
why those workers and *campesinos* are cheering you like that?"
Colombia's President Lleras Camargo asked after Kennedy
received a tumultuous welcome in the streets of Bogotá. "It's
because they believe you are on their side."

The key to Kennedy's power is that several qualities came
together in a single person, at one time, when the world was
hungry for those qualities.

First, he was a man of ideas and of ideals. It is true that he
was a man of action; a man who knew how to use power and
when not to use it. But at the core of all his actions was a deep
set of convictions and beliefs. To him freedom, racial justice,
human welfare, individual dignity were not just phrases of
casual rhetoric, but deep commitments to which he gave his
energy and ultimately his life. The people of the world sensed
this. It is easy for Americans to become cynical about the importance of ideas; to become too impressed with the importance of wealth and power. But the strength of our own country
rests upon the ideals of the small group of men who led our
Revolution. History proves that men who combine practical
action with commitment to ideals have a far more profound

and enduring impact than those who simply seek power and wealth.

Second, President Kennedy was a man of peace. Whether it was his restraint in the Cuban missile crisis or his successful efforts to secure a test ban treaty, the policies and the posture of his administration left little doubt that he desired a world where war was no longer a daily threat. And since this is what the world wants, the world's people loved him for it; and far from being afraid of American power, they felt more secure that it was in his hands.

Third, he was a man of this generation. Today 55 percent of the world's population is twenty-five or under. They saw in President Kennedy a man who had come to maturity in their time, who shared their experiences, their nearness to conflict, their hope that somehow our new knowledge could become an instrument to make life more meaningful and abundant. He was a product of today's world, and his life seemed to stretch forward into the future rather than back into the past.

Fourth, he was, in the most meaningful sense, a volunteer. He, and many others of his administration, proved that Americans are not content to sit back and idly enjoy the comforts of our abundant society. For him the commitment to public service overrode all thoughts of private pleasure or gain. He spent much of his own energy seeking to ennoble the practice of politics and the work of government, believing a great nation deserved the best of its men. In a speech just before his death he quoted Robert Frost as saying, "Nothing is true except as a man or men adhere to it—to live for it, to spend themselves on it, to die for it."

Fifth, President Kennedy cared. He cared for the hungry, the dispossessed, the despised, and the fearful. And the people of the world knew that. Much of their feeling came from his activities at home—his fight for racial justice and an end to poverty—as well as his concern for economic development and social justice abroad. They knew it not because they were acquainted with his policies or programs or read his speeches. They knew it through that curious sixth sense by which people detect compassion and concern. To them he was not a remote, commanding figure in a far-off capital, but a man whose presence and concern reached into their farms or their homes in slums. I am always taken aback when I walk into a village hut on a distant continent and find a picture of John Kennedy on the wall, torn from a newspaper and placed beside the family album or mementos.

Of course, President Kennedy's intelligence and capacity were respected and were vital to his success. But these other qualities won him his place in men's hearts. He was not a father protector, a medicine man who would solve all problems. He was a man who gave people confidence that problems could be solved and that they could solve them. He did not ask that people believe in him. He asked that people believe in themselves.

Even though it is only a few months since his death, I found around the world that there is already a growing sense of relief and gratitude that these basic beliefs and attitudes are still vigorously guiding the United States, that they will continue to help shape its policies.

In a remote area of Nepal some of our Volunteers were introduced to the local citizens as "Westerners." After they had worked there for a few months a delegation cautiously approached them and said, "You can't be Westerners. What are you?" A Volunteer answered, "We are Peace Corps Volunteers." "Oh," the Nepalese replied, "and where is Peace Corps?"

Peace Corps is right here. It is part of the real "other America" that exists somewhere underneath the tinsel, the neon signs, the racial hatred, and the poverty. It is the America we are often embarrassed to talk about unless we hide it in the

lyrics of songs, but to which in times of need we have ultimately managed to be true. If we have the courage to commit
ourselves to this America—to work for it, to believe in it—then
we may be equal to the hopes John Kennedy had for us.

2. Rediscovering the American Revolution

In the summer and fall of 1963, Sargent Shriver spoke several times on an idea rising out of his travels in fifty countries: that "wherever you go in the world, you meet the American Revolution coming back." Excerpts follow from three talks, to the Federal Bar Association in Chicago, the National Students Association Congress at Indiana University, and to the Concordia-Argonaut Club in San Francisco. At the San Francisco meeting he presented two of the first Peace Corps "veterans" who had just returned after completing their Volunteer service.

THERE IS NO QUESTION facing America more important than whether we can successfully regain the leadership of our own revolution.

U Nu, when he was Premier of Burma, asked me, "Do you really believe that a young American can compete with the Chinese Communists who have offered to come here and help us? Will your Volunteers have the same zeal for democracy that the Chinese have today for Communism?"

Like U Nu and many Americans, I have wondered whether an affluent society, with its emphasis on the organization man and the easy life, can continue to produce the self-reliance, initiative, and independence which sparked our own Revolution two centuries ago. Will Durant once observed that nations are born stoic and die epicurean. Was this happening to America? Many people thought so.

The American Revolution began as a unique movement. Its basic issues were not material but spiritual. As Jefferson and later Lincoln proclaimed, it was to be a revolution unbounded by geographical limitations; it declared the rights of all men, everywhere.

The years since the launching of that spiritual revolution have brought incredible material prosperity to its heirs. We have accumulated more wealth than any country has ever gathered at any one time in the whole history of life on this planet. But that very accumulation is alienating us from most of the people in the world who are poor, creating deep divisions at home between the insulated majority who are well-off and the isolated minority who barely subsist, and burying the deeper meaning of our society beneath a pile of steel.

"With our great wealth and power," Walter Lippmann has observed, "there should go humility, not pride. Thirty years ago this country had not only the respect and the trust but also the affection of the underdeveloped world. . . . We were not proud and self-satisfied, and we gave the effect of being in the same boat with the rest of mankind. That was when we had friends all over the world. We shall not have them again until this country becomes possessed once again . . . in the high enterprise of making a good society."

There are signs that we have become possessed once again in this endeavor. One of these signs is the vigorous pursuit of the highest goal toward which a free society can reach: equal justice for all its citizens. The determination of the Negro to win his freedom is also proving that our revolution has not yet died at home. It is an irony of democracy that a people to whom little has been given are now giving much in return. Fortunately for America, the Negro has reawakened our conscience.

When asked how justice could be secured, Solon of ancient Athens said, "Only if those who are not injured feel as indignant as those who are." Tomorrow, in the March on Washington, the world will see that thousands of Americans, white and Negro, are indignant about discrimination and injustice.

You are concerned with some of the unfinished business of America: civil rights, academic freedom, human dignity. You and other Americans are no longer satisfied simply to meet and talk about this unfinished business, not content simply to pass resolutions "expressing concern," while revolutions pass by. Now, by active participation, you can give vitality to the spirit of our country. Nowhere is that spirit more evident than among the thousands of Americans who are today assaulting the barricades of bigotry. No problem in our national life is more critically felt by our Volunteers abroad than the racial injustice that still exists here. "How can America," they are asked, "claim the name of democracy while it treats its own citizens of color unjustly?"

While the Negro is recalling some of the basic principles of our revolution at home, the Peace Corps Volunteer exemplifies it abroad. The civil rights movement and the Peace Corps both spring from the same seed and both rise toward the same hope. The kind of society the Negro is seeking here is the kind of society Peace Corps Volunteers are working to build abroad. Their spiritual kinship is attested to by the young American who said last week, "If I weren't in the Peace Corps, I would want to be a Negro." Any American who has ever wanted to become a part of the moral struggle of his generation knows what that young man meant. As Oliver Wendell Holmes said, "Life is action and passion. It is required of a man that he should share the passion and action of his time at peril of being judged not to have lived."

The action and the passion of our time—for justice and free-dom—are world-wide. And what the world wants today is our revolution. Travel in the new nations of the world, as I have over the past two years, and you will see that the revolutionary slogans scrawled on building walls and deep in the hearts of new leaders are *our* slogans: "Give me liberty or give me death!" "All men are created equal." President Sukarno of Indonesia opened the Bandung Conference of Afro-Asian people in 1955 with these words: "We are meeting on the 180th anniversary of the ride of Paul Revere. The American Revolution is the spiritual ancestor of our own revolution."

The spirit in which our Peace Corps Volunteers go forth is just as important as the skill they carry with them, for theirs is a profoundly moral challenge. They are not only being asked to help the people of these young nations achieve economic independence; they are being invited to reaffirm our own fundamental commitment to a just and free society for all peoples; they are being invited to reveal the revolutionary nature of our democratic society. More is at stake than the defeat of Communism, or the winning of new sources of wealth, or even the affection of the world's peoples. The character of American society itself is at stake.

This, the continuing American revolution at home and abroad, is what our Volunteers are discovering. The full impact may not hit them until they return home. When they do, I hope that we have a greater ability to understand the significance of these discoveries of twentieth-century explorers than did the European contemporaries and the descendants of Columbus. To them the New World, the new discovery, was a place to be exploited, an unimportant wilderness. Few could foresee the consequences which this new world would have for them. We must not make the same mistake. We cannot ignore the new world which our new discoverers are finding. Perhaps through them we can rediscover our own country. For, strange and varied as is the developing world, it is our world.

We were in at the beginning of this new world—with the shot at Concord Bridge. "The noise of that shot," Arnold Toynbee writes, "has become world-wide and it has become deafening. Jefferson hit the mark when he said that 'the disease of liberty is catching.'" But Toynbee and many others around the world think we have become immune. "America's present affluence," he writes, "has sidetracked America from the main line of the world revolution, and it has insulated her from the rest of the human race."

That is a challenge for all Americans.

3. America Discovering the World

Chulalongkorn University in Bangkok, one of the oldest and largest universities in Asia, awards honorary degrees only with the approval of Thailand's cabinet. In 1963, the cabinet decided to show its appreciation of the efforts of the 265 Peace Corps Volunteers in Thailand by awarding Sargent Shriver the degree of Doctor of Political Science—the second honorary degree ever given to a Westerner and the first in thirty-five years. It was Shriver's fifth visit to Thailand. On this occasion, January 28, 1964, Thailand's Foreign Minister called the Peace Corps "the most powerful idea in recent times."

You ARE CONCERNED with the great issues of foreign affairs. What relationship can the Peace Corps possibly have to those issues?

We might all agree that the Peace Corps has done well here in Thailand; that it has contributed to the need for skills, helped people to know more about the United States, and taught the Volunteers much about Thailand. But what of it?

In this world of the cold war and the many little hot wars, of the hydrogen bomb, the Atlantic Alliance, SEATO, and the Sino-Soviet split—on this giant Asian continent where Communist subversion, guerrilla warfare, and political uncertainty

47

occupy much of your time and thought—what room is there for a Peace Corps?

What difference can it possibly make, in the face of such enormous and complex forces that are moving the world today, that a few thousand Americans go overseas to serve mankind? Isn't it an illusion to think that the Peace Corps might actually help to bring peace, help to change the world?

Let me ask the question in a different way. What is going to change the world? If you believe men must live together in harmony in this conflict-ridden world, how is this going to come about? Guns won't change the world; that is one of the great lessons of this bloody century. Dollar bills won't change the world. Nor will simple goodwill.

What can change the world today is the same thing that has changed it in the past: an idea, and the service of dedicated individuals committed to that idea. That is how religious movements helped change the world; it is the secret of whatever power Communism had; it was the motive power of the Renaissance and the Industrial Revolution. It is the reason the American Revolution is still resounding throughout today's world. "No army," wrote Victor Hugo, "can withstand the force of an idea whose time has come." But for an idea to conquer it needs men and women who believe in it, who will work for it, who will dedicate their lives to it. The Peace Corps is a group of men and women dedicated to an idea.

Recently I was visited by an Asian official. He told me there had been more than fifty protest meetings against the Peace Corps in his country. Dozens of newspaper articles attacked us. Demands were made that his government refuse to permit our twenty-one Volunteers to land.

"Why," I asked him, "is there such concern over twenty-one Americans? You would think that we were starting germ warfare."

"In a certain sense, you are," he replied. "In my country we have more than twenty-one Americans, and if these . . . Volunteers were simply twenty-one more Americans, there would be no interest in them at all. But these Volunteers come representing an idea, the Peace Corps idea. That's why there is opposition. Your Volunteers may well infect thousands with the ideas of a free society."

In the Dominican Republic, following the recent revolution, the U.S. Government suspended economic assistance and diplomatic relations. But the Peace Corps kept on working. An experienced Latin-American newspaper correspondent sent to report on the situation wrote: "Political crises may come and go . . . but the Peace Corps has taken deep root. . . . The Peace Corps is the most radical operation which the United States has going in the Dominican Republic—no less than in the rest of Latin America."

The Peace Corps is different. It is not merely nonpolitical; it goes beyond politics and national rivalries to reach the deepest hopes of man. It is a working model, a microcosm, a small society representing the kind of world we want our children to live in.

First of all, it is a democratic society. The color of a Volunteer's skin, his religion, and his political beliefs are irrelevant. We have sent black Americans to white men's countries, white Americans to black men's countries. We were told that we couldn't send Protestants to certain parts of Catholic countries in Latin America, but we sent them. We were told that we couldn't send Jews to Arab countries, but we sent them. And in two and a half years these decisions have not cost us a moment of discontent.

Our Volunteers go overseas as free men—free to travel, to write, to read, and to speak as they please. We have built no wall of censorship or authoritarian discipline around them. And on the job they are on their own. What they accomplish is a product of their own initiative and ability and imagination.

In East Pakistan a single Volunteer, Robert Burns of St. Louis, engineered flood control works and supervised one thousand village laborers in a successful effort to overcome rising waters. For the first time in many years destructive waters were diverted from the rice fields of ten thousand families. No one told Robert Burns to begin a project which saved ten thousand families from hunger and starvation. He did it because the Peace Corps provides a framework in which individuals can use their own initiative and talents to help others. That is an important element of the Peace Corps society: reliance on the creative energies of dedicated individuals.

Nor do our Volunteers go overseas as the salesmen of a particular political theory, or economic system, or religious creed. They go to work *with* people, not to employ them, use them, or advise them. They do what the country they go to *wants them to do,* not what we think is best. They live among the people, sharing their homes, eating their food, talking their language, living under their laws, not in special compounds with special privileges.

But if the Volunteer is not a salesman, neither is he a man without a mission. He goes overseas not merely as a willing and a skilled worker, but as a representative, a living example, of the most powerful idea of all: the idea that free and committed men and women can cross, even transcend, boundaries of culture and language, of alien tradition and great disparities of wealth, of old hostilities and new nationalisms, to meet with other men and women on the common ground of service to human welfare and human dignity.

It will require many years, and a much greater effort, for this idea to succeed, not only by the Peace Corps, but by other men and institutions in all countries. But the impact we have had so far has given a faint glimmer, a shadow no bigger than a man's hand, of the possibilities of the future.

In Ghana approximately one-third of all degree-holding instructors in the secondary schools are Peace Corps Volunteers. In Ethiopia and Nyasaland a third of all the secondary school teachers are Volunteers. In Sierra Leone more than half of all the qualified teachers are Volunteers—more than the British supplied when Sierra Leone was a colony. And the Volunteers are in all these places by invitation, not by conquest.

Perhaps the greatest testimony to the impact of the Peace Corps, the sincerest form of flattery, is the fact that other Western nations are following our lead. In the past year nearly every European country has expanded or established Peace Corps programs of their own.

But the work the Peace Corps is doing abroad is only part, and perhaps not the most important part, of the Peace Corps story.

In terms of the history of your civilization it is a short time since the world discovered America. But it is now, and in good part through the Peace Corps Volunteers, that America is discovering the world.

They are not discovering the world of history books and maps, of the tourist brochure, the guided tour, and the movie travelogue. It is not the world of the big cities and the important people. The world they are discovering, in their thousands of villages, is a different world.

It is a world of rich diversity—diversity of problems, of customs, of traditions, of values, of wisdom. An American Volunteer in Nigeria who finds himself treated with respect and friendship although he is a white man in a black man's country has learned that the world has much to teach us about racial matters. The Volunteer here in Thailand who has had the chance to observe the patient and wise dignity of your people learns about important values which are all too rare in America.

And as the Volunteer comes to know and respect and learn from the varied customs and institutions of different peoples, he also comes to see the strain of human unity which runs underneath. "For the last four months," wrote one Volunteer, "I lived with a Filipino family who were my friends and companions. I soon forgot that I was an American and they were Filipinos. They treated me as one of the family. All of us, as human beings, have the same basic needs and desires and a common yearning to be understood and respected."

Our Volunteers are also discovering the basic facts of life in the developing world—a world which, for all its richness of culture, is living often on the edge of survival. These facts are well known to you. You live surrounded by them every day. But to Americans, imprisoned in their remote affluence, there is little chance to appreciate the realities of life in much of the world. Our Volunteers are coming to understand these realities. "People die here for want of so little," wrote one Volunteer from East Africa.

Volunteers have also discovered a world in which there are few simple answers. Those who think there are panaceas for the ills of emerging nations, who believe that all we need is more money or more schools or more democracy or more private enterprise, have never served in the Peace Corps.

But despite the difficulties, the complexity of problems and the depth of frustrations, the Volunteer is also discovering a world where something is happening, a world which is going somewhere. This is often described as the "Revolution of Rising Expectations." But this is just a phrase. The Peace Corps is discovering, at first hand, what those words mean. Volunteers are experiencing the satisfaction of helping to meet this Revolution of Rising Expectations. This is revolution in the most modern sense—not a revolution of rulers but of the ruled, not just a revolution for power but for progress, not a revolution in government, but a revolution in civilization.

This is some of the world our Volunteers are discovering on this new voyage of discovery known as the Peace Corps. When they return, taking their places in our schools and government, industry and business, they will give us a far better knowledge of the richness, the difficulties, and the dangers in the world around us.

And so here in Thailand, and in all the other countries in which we serve, it is America which is benefiting from the Peace Corps. It is we who probably learn and profit the most. And for the opportunity we are grateful to your country.

4. "Go Up-Country to Find the Hidden Heart"

Under the chairmanship of Lyndon Johnson, delegates from forty-three nations met in Puerto Rico in October 1962 to attend the International Conference on Middle-Level Manpower. Cabinet members came from both industrialized and newly developing nations to discuss new ways to provide the skilled manpower so sorely missed by the new nations. They unanimously established an International Peace Corps Secretariat to assist in the organization of volunteer programs by participating countries. As the initiator and organizer of the Conference, Sargent Shriver spoke on the special vision of foreign people and foreign lands gained by working Volunteers.

THE SIGNIFICANCE OF THE PEACE CORPS goes far beyond the number of Volunteers in service or the number of countries in which they work. For an explanation of the Peace Corps' true significance we must look to the mainstream of the American tradition.

Let us admit that we have not always been true to this tradition. We have not always supported freedom abroad nor fully realized it at home. We have sometimes failed to understand the aspirations of people in other lands or to fulfill the hopes of our own people. Yet throughout our history we have retained an underlying dedication to certain principles. We regard our lapses from these principles as temporary aberrations, mistakes, departures from what America should be and should stand for. It is because the men and women of the Peace Corps inherit these beliefs, because they have absorbed them in the schoolrooms and churches, that they have been able to cross barriers of language and culture, religious faith and social structure, to touch the deep chords of common hope and principle which belong to all men.

The first of these principles is the conviction that the goals of the American Revolution against colonial rule were universal goals. We were not simply fighting for American values; we were part of the greater revolution of man as he struggles to be free. Said Thomas Jefferson, "Every man and every body of men on earth possesses the right of self-government. They receive it with their being from the hand of nature." There are those who scorn such simple words as "freedom," "self-government," "the rights of man" as too simple and superficial for our complex, modern age. On the contrary, these words represent the basic revolutionary forces which are reshaping all continents.

The second of these principles is our belief in the world's right to diversity. We built a country out of many lands and from people of a hundred different backgrounds and faiths. John Kennedy's grandfather was an immigrant to Boston. President Dwight Eisenhower came from the rural heartland of America. Our original states warred against each other for commerce and territory. And today there are still frictions and difficulties between regions and faiths and colors. But whatever success we have had in building a free nation stems from our confidence in a society which contains many societies. Our strength lies in the richness of our differences. And thus we do not fear the liberating discords of a diversified world society. We welcome what Gandhi called "the creative interdependence" of different lands.

The third of these principles is the belief in the power of individual moral conscience to remake the world—the belief so well expressed by men like Thoreau, that man has a higher duty than his obligation to party or state: a duty to conscience and common humanity. "Freedom is really in the mind," says Sierra Leone's poet, Abioseh Nicol. In the last analysis it is not governments or organizations which will give fruition to man's hopes, but the energies and talents of millions of individuals working across national borders and dedicated to the service of mankind.

The last of these principles is man's optimism—the belief that all things are possible to men of determination and energy and a willingness to toil. This confidence came naturally to those who threw off the bonds of colonial rule and succeeded, with their own efforts, in subduing a wild and rich continent. But the same sense of man's limitless capacity is also moving now in Africa, in Asia, in Europe, and in Latin America.

It is because our Volunteers believe in these principles that they welcome the opportunity to help others. We were in danger of losing our way among the television sets, the supermarkets, and the material abundance of a rich society. Our debt of gratitude to the developing and emerging nations of the world is that they have reminded us of our own traditions, and given us a treasured opportunity to sacrifice and work once more for those principles which created our own nation. By letting us participate in their struggles they have given us a chance to find ourselves.

These are not just American doctrines. They belong to all lands and to all people. They are fundamental human beliefs. On them rests the strength of nations. If from time to time any of us has momentarily lost sight of them, they have nonetheless remained at the moral heart of the universe. They have now stirred us to action in sending out thousands of Americans dedicated on a world scale to the same cause which built their nation. As this helps others to build their societies, it helps us to strengthen our own. And we welcome the swelling chorus of announcements that numerous other countries will begin Peace Corps efforts of their own.

As American astronaut John Glenn recently said of our efforts in space, "We shall be relying more and more on international teamwork. We have an infinite amount to learn both from nature and from each other." These are hopes that must be realized on earth no less than in outer space. The development of nations is the process of developing men, a process in which we have an infinite amount to learn from nature and from each other. The Peace Corps is part of this process.

Abioseh Nicol has written:

> Go up-country, they said,
> To see the real Africa. . . .
>
> You will find your hidden heart,
> Your mute ancestral spirit.*

Peace Corps Volunteers have gone up-country to live and work, and they are seeing the real Africa and the real Asia and the real Latin America. They will return to the United States with the profound and enlightening experience of having lived among the people of foreign lands, not as "expatriates," but as persons who have eaten their food, lived in their houses, lived under their laws, spoken their languages, and shared their work. They will have a new understanding of the aspirations and the wants of the people with whom they share this turbulent globe an understanding not gleaned from books or newspapers or hurried trips to capital cities, but the deep understanding which

* From "Up-Country," in *An African Treasury*, edited by Langston Hughes. Copyright © 1960 by Langston Hughes. Reprinted by permission of Crown Publishers, Inc.

can only come from being a genuine part of the society one seeks to know. Wherever they go they will enrich the life of their communities. They will help create an America more profoundly aware of world problems and world responsibilities.

5. War and Poverty

In the following excerpts from his convocation address to some five thousand students and faculty of Texas Technological College, in Lubbock, Texas, on April 9, 1964, Sargent Shriver discussed the connections between his two assignments, the Peace Corps and the War on Poverty.

THE GREAT FACT OF WORLD LIFE is that for the first time it is possible for the benefits of science and technology to be made available to all men. We have the means to end poverty at home and to help those in the world seeking a decent life. You know we have the means, especially you who are studying our modern science and technology, you who know the modern miracles that can be performed. You know this, and the world knows it. Having the means to end poverty and to create the conditions of peace in the world, it follows that we have the duty to do it. And that is the heart of the problem of establishing peace and ending poverty: Can we, the richest and most powerful people on earth, can we who have been so blessed, bring out the best within us to do what we know we ought to do?

If we fail to do enough, if it is the old story of too little too late, then our whole civilization may go down. The historian

59

Arnold Toynbee says that all twenty previous civilizations have collapsed because they failed to solve the twin problems of war and poverty.

The news is out now, and people everywhere are coming to believe that they no longer need be poor forever. Governments and civilizations fall when they fail to act to provide opportunity for all citizens. Most of the violent revolutions of our time rise out of such failures. The result of inaction is chaos or Communism, and war.

In the case of the Peace Corps, this country fortunately acted first, instead of waiting for others to act and then reacting. What if the Kremlin or Peking had acted first?

What if our newspapers were reporting that a Soviet or a Chinese Peace Corps, soon to be ten thousand strong, had been welcomed into, asked into, forty-six countries, that ten thousand dedicated young Communists were working in the schools, hospitals, and villages of Asia, Africa, and Latin America at the invitation of host governments? What if the next generation of many countries were being taught by friendly, hard-working, simple-living members of a Soviet Peace Corps? What a Congressional investigation we would have then!

We do not need to worry, because this is the one thing Mr. Khrushchev doesn't dare to do: let his young men and women go and see and live in and learn about the world beyond the wall. They can be permitted to undertake propaganda missions or to live in embassy compounds. But he does not trust them to work and serve by themselves, on their own, in the schools and in the homes of proud and independent peoples.

Maybe it would be good for all of us if Soviet youth could get a chance to see the outside world on a large scale. The ideas they would take home, the questions they would ask, might bring about or speed up a peaceful change within Soviet society.

America was able to launch the Peace Corps, to trust its young people, to let you loose in the world to work, to question, to teach, and to learn, because freedom is our first principle, because individual initiative is our secret weapon.

Now President Johnson is determined to make a breakthrough in the struggle against poverty. With the proposed Job Corps and a corps of volunteers to serve in America, with the community action programs and other measures before Congress, we are going to make a frontal attack on poverty. With the Peace Corps, we have shown how Americans, young in spirit, can turn an idea into action, a dream into reality. We can do the same in the War on Poverty.

President Johnson declared this a *war* against poverty in order to mobilize the full will of America. In war, we give everything we have. For peace in the world and full opportunity at home, we need to give more of ourselves, as we would in war.

We do not yet know all that needs to be known about the job ahead. We do not know how to go to the moon yet either, but we are going to get there. Fifty years ago, we did not know how to eliminate typhoid fever, scarlet fever, whooping cough, diphtheria, or paralytic polio. But we found out. Twenty-five years ago, we didn't know how to split the atom, but we found out. We may not yet know exactly how to go about ending poverty and abolishing war, but we are going to find out.

In John Kennedy's words, "All this will not be finished in the first one hundred days. Nor will it be finished in the first one thousand days, nor in the life of this Administration, nor even perhaps in our lifetime on this planet. But let us begin."

III

THE

PEACE

CORPS

"Here is a movement whose express purpose
is to overcome the disastrous barriers that have
hitherto segregated the affluent Western minority of
the human race from the majority of their fellow men
and women. I believe that, in the Peace Corps, the
non-Western majority of mankind is going to meet a
sample of Western man at his best."
— ARNOLD TOYNBEE

In the early days of the Peace Corps, an indiscreet postcard home by a Volunteer named Margery Michelmore was found by Nigerian students and caused a flurry of protests. This unfortunate incident confirmed the doubts of many Americans about the wisdom of the program.

Fortunately, Congress, with its closeness to the people and its understanding of American politics, saw the common sense of the Peace Corps idea and did not abandon hope in the Peace Corps Volunteers because of one mishap. Nor did the Nigerian Government or people withdraw their support of the new experiment. Since Margery Michelmore's first group of 37 Volunteers, eight new groups totaling over 600 Volunteers have been invited by the Nigerian Government and warmly received by the Nigerian people.

Some say that the tide of Nigerian opinion turned favorable when one of the first Volunteers saved the life of a drowning Nigerian by mouth-to-mouth resuscitation. But dramatic incidents, even symbolic acts, do not count as much as the quiet work, the daily drudgery of Volunteers on the job.

Pericles called ancient Athens the School of Hellas. The Peace Corps is a School of America. As the following reports and talks suggest, this is in the best American tradition of learning by doing.

1. Two Years of the Peace Corps

This piece discussing some of the problems faced in the first two years was adapted from an article written for Foreign Affairs, *July 1963.*

OSCAR WILDE IS SAID to have observed that America really was discovered by a dozen people before Columbus, but it was always successfully hushed up. I am tempted to feel that way about the Peace Corps. The idea of a national effort of this type had been proposed many times in past years, but in 1960 and 1961 for the first time the idea was joined with the power and the desire to implement it.

An organization, we know, gains life through hard decisions, so we hammered out basic policies in long, detailed discussions in which we sought to face up to the practical problems and reach specific solutions before we actually started operations. We knew that a few wrong judgments in the early hours of a new organization's life, especially a controversial government agency, can completely thwart its purposes, even as a margin of error of a thousandth of an inch in the launching of a rocket can send it thousands of miles off course. We knew, too, that a thousand suspicious eyes were peering over our shoulders. Some were the eyes of friendly critics, but many belonged to unfriendly skeptics. The youthfulness of the new administration, particularly of the President, enhanced the risk; an older leadership would have had greater immunity to charges of "sophomorism."

Even the choice of a name took on serious overtones. The phrase "Peace Corps" was used in Kennedy's San Francisco campaign speech, when he formally presented the idea for such a program, but many of our advisers disliked it. "Peace," they claimed, was a word the Communists had pre-empted, and "Corps" carried undesirable military connotations. We did not want a name contrived out of initials which a public relations firm might have devised; nor did we want to restrict participation in the program by calling it a "Youth Corps." What we did want was a name which the public at large could grasp emotionally as well as intellectually. Whatever name we did choose, we would give it content by our acts and programs. We wanted it, also, to reflect the seriousness of our objectives. We studied dozens of other names and finally came back to the original. Peace is the fundamental goal of our times. We believed the Peace Corps could contribute to its attainment.

The ambitiousness of the name, of course, was only one reason for early skepticism about the Peace Corps. Fears were voiced that it might be a "second children's crusade." I was astonished that a nation so young had become so suspicious of its youth. We had forgotten that Thomas Jefferson drafted the Declaration of Independence at age thirty-three. Forgotten also was the fact that more than half of the world's population is under twenty-six, the age of the average Peace Corps Volunteer. Sixteen of the nations in Africa have heads of state under forty-five; five have leaders in their thirties.

Of course, youthful enthusiasm and noble purposes were not enough. They had to be combined with hard-headed pragmatism and realistic administration. In the early days of the Peace Corps we were looking for a formula for practical idealism. The formula worked out by experience has "the sweet smell of success" today, but it was far less clear two years ago.

Would enough qualified Americans be willing to serve? Even if they started, would they be able to continue on the job despite frustration, dysentery, and boredom? Could Americans survive overseas without special foods and privileges, special housing, automobiles, television, and air conditioners? Many Americans thought not. The Washington correspondent of the respected *Times of India* agreed with them in these words:

When you have ascertained a felt local need, you would need to find an American who can exactly help in meeting it. This implies not only the wherewithal (or what you inelegantly call the "know how") but also a psychological affinity with a strange new people who may be illiterate and yet not lack Wisdom, who may live in hovels and yet dwell in spiritual splendor, who may be poor in worldly wealth and yet enjoy a wealth of intangibles and a capacity to be happy. Would an American young man be in tune with this world he has never experienced before? I doubt it. . . .

One also wonders whether American young men and tender young girls, reared in air-conditioned houses at a constant temperature, knowing little about the severities of nature (except when they pop in and out of cars or buses), will be able to suffer the Indian summer smilingly and, if they go into an Indian village, whether they will be able to sleep on unsprung beds under the canopy of the bejeweled sky or indoors in mud huts, without writing home about it.

At a time when many were saying that Americans had gone soft and were interested mainly in security, pensions, and suburbia, the Peace Corps could have been timorous. Possible ways of hedging against an anticipated shortage of applicants could have included low qualification standards, generous inducements to service, cautious programming, a period of duty shorter than two years, an enforced period of enlistment such as the "hitch" in the armed forces, or draft exemption for volunteer service in the Peace Corps. We deliberately chose the risk rather than the hedge in each case and created an obstacle course. The applicant could remove himself any time he realized his motive was less than a true desire for service. This method of self-selection has by now saved us from compounded difficulties abroad.

Our optimism about sufficient recruits was justified. More than fifty thousand Americans have applied for the Peace Corps. [*By the summer of 1964 over one hundred thousand had applied.* Ed. note.] In the first three months of this year, more Americans applied for the Peace Corps than were drafted for military service. This happened notwithstanding the fact that young men who volunteer for the Peace Corps are liable to service on their return.

Selection was made rigorous. The process was fashioned to include a searchingly thorough application form, placement tests to measure useful skills, language aptitude exams, six to twelve reference inquiries, a suitability investigation, and systematic observation of performance during the training program of approximately ten weeks. We invite about one in six applicants to enter training, and about five out of six trainees are finally selected for overseas service.

We debated hotly the question of age, and whether or not older people should be eligible. We listened to proposals for an age limit in the thirties and then in the sixties and finally decided to set no upper age limit at all. Our oldest Volunteer today happens to be seventy-six, and we have more grandparents than teen-agers in the Peace Corps. Some older Volunteers have turned out to be rigid and cantankerous in adapting to a standard of living *their* parents took for granted, but the majority of them make a lot of us on the New Frontier look like stodgy old settlers.

From the beginning we decided that effective volunteers abroad would need systematic administrative support and direction. Leaders of several developing nations, eager to have the assistance of trained manpower, warned against repeating the experiences of other highly motivated volunteer workers who had failed abroad for lack of cohesive leadership. A good program would need good people, not only as Peace Corps Volunteers, but as Peace Corps staff members abroad. There was no counterpart in the U.S. Government of civilian leaders serving abroad on a volunteer basis. There was no precedent for what these men would have to do in programming, logistics, and personal support for the Volunteers in their charge. We needed the ablest of leaders in each position. Could we attract them even though we did not offer post differentials, cost-of-living allowances, commissary or diplomatic privileges?

Fortunately, the answer has been a continuing "Yes." The Peace Corps has attracted intelligent and dedicated men to all positions on its overseas team. Ironically, the same critics who once complained that we would unleash hordes of uninstructed adolescents on the world are now complaining that we spend substantial sums to provide instruction and adequate direction.

Some of my colleagues proposed that Peace Corps Volunteers act as technical helpers to AID (Agency for International Development) technicians, "extra hands" for the more experienced older men. Peace Corps practice has moved in another direction. A natural distinction between the AID adviser at a high level in government and the Peace Corps Volunteer making his contribution as a "doer" or "worker" at the grass roots soon became apparent. It also became clear that the Peace Corps Volunteer had a new and perhaps unique contribution to make as a person who entered fully into host-country life and institutions, with a host-country national working beside him, and another directing his work. This feature of the Peace Corps contributed substantially to its early support abroad.

Discussion of the possibility that the Peace Corps might be affiliated with the AID led into the question of its relationship to U.S. political and information establishments overseas. The Peace Corps in Washington is responsible to the Secretary of State. Volunteers and staff abroad are responsible to the American ambassador. Nevertheless, the Peace Corps maintains a distinction between its functions and those of embassies, AID and USIA offices. There was a design to this which Secretary Rusk has aptly described: "The Peace Corps is not an instrument *of* foreign policy, because to make it so would rob it of its contribution *to* foreign policy."

Peace Corps Volunteers are not trained diplomats; they are not propagandists; they are not technical experts. They represent our society by what they are, what they do, and the spirit in which they do it. They steer clear of intelligence activity and stay out of local politics. Our strict adherence to these principles has been a crucial factor in the decision of politically uncommitted countries to invite American Volunteers into their midst, into their homes, and even into their classrooms and school yards to teach future generations of national leaders. In an era of sabotage and espionage, intelligence and counterintelligence, the Peace Corps and its Volunteers have earned a priceless yet simple renown: they are trustworthy.

Another contested issue in the early days of the Peace Corps concerned private organizations and universities. We were advised by many to make grants to these institutions, then to leave recruitment, selection, training, and overseas programming in their hands. That road would have led to an organization operating very much like the National Science Foundation. For better or worse, the Peace Corps chose not to become a grant-making organization, and those decisions which give character to our operations—selection, training, programming, field leadership, and so on—are still in our possession.

Nevertheless, the involvement of private organizations and universities has been crucial to the Peace Corps' success. America is a pluralistic society, and the Peace Corps expresses its diversity abroad by demonstrating that the public and private sectors can work cooperatively and effectively. We consciously seek contracts with private organizations, colleges, and universities to administer our programs. We gain the advantage of expert knowledge, long experience, tested working relationships, and often even private material resources. For example, CARE has contributed more than $100,000 worth of equipment to the Peace Corps in Colombia. Initially, there was suspicion by some of these agencies that the Peace Corps, with the resources of the United States taxpayer behind it, would pre-empt their own work abroad. Suspicion has turned into understanding, however, as the United States Government, through the Peace Corps, has facilitated the work of private organizations and has focused new attention on the needs and opportunities for service abroad.

In our "talent search" we went to government, academic life, business, the bar, the medical profession, and every other walk of life where leadership was available. We deliberately recruited as many Negroes and representatives of other minority groups as possible for jobs in every echelon. We knew that Negroes would not ordinarily apply for high-level policy jobs, so we decided to seek them out. Today 7.4 percent of our higher-echelon positions are filled by Negroes as compared to 0.8 percent for other government agencies in similar grades; 24 percent of our other positions are filled by Negroes, compared to a figure for government agencies in general of 5.5 percent.

How big should the Peace Corps be? Everyone was asking this question and everyone had an answer. Advice ranged from five hundred to one million. There were strong voices raised in support of "tentative pilot projects," looking to a Peace Corps of less than one thousand. However, Warren W. Wiggins, an experienced foreign-aid expert, took a broader view. He pointed out that ultracautious programming might produce prohibitive per capita costs, fail even to engage the attention of responsible foreign officials (let alone have an impact), and fail to attract the necessary American talent and commitment. Furthermore, when the need was insatiable, why should we try to meet it with a pittance?

There were also arguments in those early days about "saturation" of the foreign country, either in terms of jobs or the psychological impact of the American presence. I have since noticed that the same arguments made about a 500-1,000 man program in 1961 were also made about our plans to expand to 5,000 Volunteers (March, 1963), to 10,000 Volunteers (March, 1964). I am not suggesting that the Peace Corps should continue to grow indefinitely. But I am proposing that much time and energy are wasted in theoretical musings, introspections, and worries about the future. Peace Corps Volunteers are a new type of overseas American. Who is to say now how many of them will be welcome abroad next year, or in the next decade? Our country and our times have had plenty of experience with programs that were too little, too late.

The question of the health of the Volunteers concerned us from the beginning. The Peace Corps represents the largest group of Americans who have ever tried to live abroad "up-country." Even in World War II our troops were generally in organized units where safe food and water could be provided and medical care was at hand. This would not be the case for the Peace Corps. And an incapacitated Volunteer would probably be worse than no Volunteer at all. How could we reduce the risks to a rational level? The Surgeon General studied the problem at our request. We then worked out a solution by which preventive health measures are provided by Public Health doctors assigned to the Peace Corps, while much of the actual medical care is handled by doctors of the host country. Of the first 117 Volunteers returned to the United States, only 20 came back for medical reasons (21 returned for compassionate reasons, 71 failed to adjust to overseas living, and 5 died or were killed in accidents). Our medical division's work is already showing up in the pages of scientific and medical journals. As an example, we recently decided to use large injections of gamma globulin as a preventive for hepatitis, which has presented one of the worst health problems for Americans overseas. Since then, there has not been a single case of infectious hepatitis reported among those who received the large injection in time.

Many of the original doubts and criticisms of the Peace Corps have not materialized. On the other hand, substantive problems have emerged which were little discussed or expected two years ago. One of the most difficult is the provision of adequate language training. This was foreseen, but most observers thought that the exotic languages such as Thai, Urdu, Bengali, and Twi would give us our main problem, while Spanish and French speakers could be easily recruited or quickly trained. The opposite has been true. The first Volunteers who arrived in Thailand in January 1962 made a great impression with what observers described as "fluent" Thai. As the Volunteers were the first to point out, their Thai was not actually fluent, but their modest achievement was tremendously appreciated. Since then, of course, a large proportion of the Volunteers there have become truly fluent.

On the other hand, a considerable number of Volunteers going to Latin America and to French Africa have been criticized for their mediocre language fluency. Expectations are high in these countries, and halting Spanish or French is not enough. We have learned that America contains rather few French-speaking bus mechanics, Spanish-speaking hydrologists, or math-science teachers who can explain theorems in a Latin-American classroom. Can we devise more effective and intensive language training, particularly for farmers, craftsmen, construction foremen, well drillers, and other Americans who never before have needed a second language? Should we take skilled people and teach them languages or take people with language abilities and teach them skills?

We still need more Volunteers, especially those who combine motivation and special skills. The person with a ready motivation for Peace Corps service tends to be the liberal arts student in college, the social scientist, the person with "human relations" interests. The developing countries need and want a great many Americans with this background, but they also want engineers, agronomists, lathe operators, and geologists. We cannot make our maximum contribution if we turn down requests for skills which we have difficulty finding. There are presently 61 engineers in the Peace Corps, 30 geologists, and 236 nurses, respectable numbers considering the ready availability of generously paying jobs in the domestic economy. But requests still far outnumber the supply.

Earlier I mentioned there has been a change in the nature of comment and criticism about the Peace Corps. In the beginning, the doubters worried about the callowness of youth and the ability of mortals to make any good idea work. The more recent criticism is more sophisticated and more substantive. Eric Sevareid recently observed: "While the Corps has something to do with spot benefits in a few isolated places, whether in sanitizing drinking water or building culverts, its work has, and can have, very little to do with the fundamental investments, reorganizations and reforms upon which the true and long-term economic development of backward countries depends." Mr. Sevareid acknowledges that "giving frustrated American youth a sense of mission and adding to our supply of comprehension of other societies fatten the credit side of the ledger." He adds: "If fringe benefits were all the Corps' originators had in mind, then this should be made clear to the country."

I do not agree with him that the second and third purposes

of the Peace Corps Act—representing America abroad in the best sense and giving Americans an opportunity to learn about other societies—are "fringe benefits." Fulton Freeman, the United States Ambassador in Colombia, believes the whole Peace Corps program could be justified by its creation of a new American resource in the Volunteers who are acquiring language skills and intensive understanding of a foreign society. Former Volunteers will be entering government service, United Nations agencies, academic life, international business concerns, and a host of other institutions which carry on the business of the United States throughout the world. Others will return to their homes, capable of exerting an enlightened influence in the communities where they settle. Many trite euphemisms of the ignorant and ready panaceas of the uniformed will clash immediately with the harsh facts that Volunteers have learned to live with abroad.

Is the second purpose of the Peace Corps Act—to be a good representative of our society abroad—a "fringe benefit"? A Peace Corps Volunteer reaches the people of foreign countries on an individual basis. He leaves to the diplomat and the technician the complex tools which are peculiarly their own while he sets out to work in the local environment as he finds it.

I am not suggesting that life for the Volunteer is always hard. A visiting Ghanaian said, "The Peace Corps teachers in my country don't live so badly. After all, they live as well as we do." I agree that this is not so bad. Nor is our objective discomfort for discomfort's sake, but rather a willingness to share the life of another people, to accept sacrifice when sacrifice is necessary, and to show that material privilege has not become the central and indispensable ingredient in an American's life. It is interesting to note that the happiest Volunteers are usually those with the most difficult living conditions.

Although I disagree with Mr. Sevareid's emphasis in dismissing two of the three purposes of the Peace Corps Act as "fringe benefits," he does get to the heart of an important question when he compares the direct economic impact of the Peace Corps to fundamental investments, reorganizations, and economic development. The Peace Corps' contribution has been less in direct economic development than in social development —health, education, construction, and community organization. We are convinced that economic development directly depends on social development. In his valedictory report this past April as head of the Economic Commission for Latin America, Raúl Prebisch observed that there are *not* "grounds for expecting that economic development will take place first and be followed in the natural course of events by social development. Both social and economic development must be achieved in measures that require the exercise of rational and deliberate action. . . . There can be no speed-up in economic development without a change in the social structure." While they have their differences, Theodore W. Schultz and J. Kenneth Galbraith have no disagreement on the essential role of social development in economic progress. In contrast, some who argue from the European–North American experience overlook the vital need for social development which had already been substantially achieved in the countries of the Atlantic community. This is the basic difference between the problem of the Marshall Plan, which was concerned with economic reconstruction in societies with abundant social resources, and the problem of forced-draft economic development in much of Asia, Africa, and Latin America.

Notwithstanding the Peace Corps' primary emphasis on social development, Volunteers are making a direct economic contribution in a variety of situations. They are helping to organize farmers' cooperatives in Chile, Ecuador, and Pakistan; credit unions and savings and loan associations in Latin America; demonstration farms in the Near East. A group of Volunteers in the Punjab sparked the creation of a poultry industry of some economic significance. These are "grass-roots" projects. More of them will someday cause us to look back and wonder why it took so long to discover that people—human hands and enthusiasms—are an essential part of the relationship of mutual assistance which we must establish with our neighbors abroad.

The Peace Corps is not a "foreign aid" agency. Two of the three purposes of the Peace Corps as defined in the Act deal with understanding, not economic assistance. Moreover, our financial investment is in the Volunteer, who brings his skills and knowledge home with him. Seventy-five percent of the Peace Corps' appropriated funds enters the economy of the United States; of the remaining 25 percent, more than half (57 percent) is spent on American citizens, the Peace Corps Volunteers themselves.

Two countries, Ghana and Argentina, have expressed interest in making the Peace Corps a two-way street by sending volunteer teachers of special competence to interested American high schools or colleges. Ghana would provide experts in African history and Argentina teachers of Spanish. Other countries may follow suit.

Our own Peace Corps Volunteers are being changed in the acquisition of languages and expertise. They will be coming home more mature, with a new outlook toward life and work. The Peace Corps is truly a new frontier in the sense that it provides the challenge to self-reliance and independent action which the vanished frontier once provided on our own continent.

The influence of the Peace Corps idea might be described as a series of widening circles, like the expanding rings from a stone thrown into a pond. The inner, most sharply defined circle represents the immediate effect of the program: accomplishments abroad in social and economic development, skills, knowledge, understanding, institution-building, a framework for cooperative effort with private organizations, research and experiment in "overseas Americanship," language training, and improvements in health.

The second ring moving outward on the water might be the Peace Corps' influence on our society, on institutions and people, on the creation of a new sense of participation in world events, an influence on the national sense of purpose, self-reliance, and an expanded concept of volunteer service in time of peace.

There is still a wider circle and, being farthest from the splash, the hardest to make out clearly. Perhaps I can explain it by describing the relationships I see between the Peace Corps and our American Revolution. The Revolution placed on our citizens the responsibility for reordering their own social structure. It was a triumph over the idea that man is incompetent or incapable of shaping his destiny. It was our declaration of the irresistible strength of a universal idea connected with human dignity, hope, compassion, and freedom. The idea was not simply American, of course, but arose from a confluence of history, geography, and the genius of a resolute few at Philadelphia.

We still have our vision, but our society has been drifting away from the world's majority: the young and raw, the colored, the hungry, and the oppressed. The Peace Corps is helping to put us again where we belong. It is our newest hope for rejoining the majority of the world.

2. An International Movement

To the Hadassah Convention, in Washington, D.C., on October 28, 1963, Sargent Shriver spoke on the significant but unreported work of the International Peace Corps Secretariat, which has successfully assisted in the creation of Peace Corps-type operations in eight countries and is now working with another twenty-four countries. In 1964 it adopted a new and broader name to facilitate its further expansion: the International Secretariat for Volunteer Services.

ONE OF THE BIGGEST unreported Peace Corps stories is not about the United States Peace Corps at all. It is about the spread of the Peace Corps movement, the Peace Corps idea, across the free world. It is the opening of a brand-new frontier of voluntary service. It all began with a meeting, a convention much like this one.

In the Peace Corps we were impressed with the contribution which skilled volunteers could make to the progress of countries emerging from centuries of poverty. We had found that foreign aid and local investment could not do the job without the skilled men and women needed to put that money to work —to teach in schools, to improve agriculture, to man the factories and the institutions of government. We had seen that without man money alone was helpless to improve human wel-

81

fare. Of course, this is not news to this organization. For the wealth of human resources—skills, talents, and intelligence— has been the major secret, the hidden weapon, of the amazing progress of the State of Israel.

So just a year ago this month, the Peace Corps sponsored a conference of forty-three nations in Puerto Rico. The major purpose of the conference was to examine ways in which skilled volunteers could be used more widely and more effectively to help solve the most urgent human needs of the developing countries. To this conference came three vice presidents—including our own—ministers and cabinet officers from all over the world.

The conference established the International Peace Corps Secretariat—a Secretariat whose purpose, unanimously agreed upon, was to encourage and assist the spread of the volunteer movement, the Peace Corps idea, throughout the world.

The work of the International Peace Corps Secretariat over the past year is proof that for the Peace Corps idea the time had come.

It is not the purpose of this Secretariat to "internationalize" the United States Peace Corps, to form a supranational organization responsible for volunteers from different countries. Its only function is to help and encourage other national Peace Corps like our own, responsible to their own governments and people.

Its success is one of the little-known stories of the year. For almost every industrialized country in the free world has begun to establish its own version of the Peace Corps.

The Netherlands Volunteer Corps is already in training for work in the Cameroons, with another group scheduled for northeast Brazil. Danish volunteers have begun work in Tanganyika. The German Peace Corps, the German Development Service, was inaugurated a few months ago in a ceremony with President Luebke, Chancellor Adenauer, and President Ken-

Sargent Shriver was sworn in as Director of the Peace Corps by Supreme Court Justice William O. Douglas in the presence of Vice President Lyndon B. Johnson and Secretary of State Dean Rusk.

When President John F. Kennedy signed the Peace Corps Act, September 22, 1961, one of the pens went to his brother-in-law, the Director of the Corps. (Below) Harry Belafonte and Dr. Benjamin Mays with Mr. Shriver at the first meeting of the Peace Corps Advisory Council.

Sargent Shriver and the members of President Johnson's task force at a planning session for the War on Poverty.

On a world trip in 1961, Mr. Shriver conferred with President Sekou Touré of the Republic of Guinea (above) and U Ko Gyi (below), director of the Burmese Agricultural and Rural Development Corporation.

(U.S.I.S. Photo)

(U.S.I.S. [India] Photo)

He discussed community development with a Punjabi official in India (above) and an official in the Philippines (below).

(ICA Photo)

(Photo by Rowland Scherman, Peace Corps)

Mr. Shriver appeared with President John F. Kennedy at the White House in August, 1961, when President Kennedy addressed eighty Ghana and Tanganyika Peace Corps Volunteers—the first Volunteers to go overseas.

Eunice Kennedy Shriver and her husband working on Kennedy Foundation medical programs.

In January, 1964, Mr. Shriver met with Patriarch Athenagoras in Istanbul (left) and with former Prime Minister David Ben-Gurion in Israel (below).

(Photos by Paul Conklin)

(Photo by Paul Conklin)

He delivered a message from President Johnson to Pope Paul VI in Jerusalem.

(Photo by Paul Conklin)

In Teheran, January, 1964, Sargent Shriver helped to dedicate a John F. Kennedy Avenue. He is shown after the ceremony with Iranian Prime Minister Assadolah Alam.

(Photo by Paul Conklin)

He delivered letters from President Johnson to King Hussein of Jordan (above) and King Mahendra of Nepal (below).

(Photo by Paul Conklin)

(Photo by Paul Conklin)

In Bangkok Mr. Shriver was awarded an honorary doctorate by Chulalongkorn University. On the stage he sat between Foreign Minister Thanat Khoman and Prime Minister Thanom Kittikachorn of Thailand. (Below) In India with U.S. Ambassador Chester Bowles he talked with President Radhakrishnan.

(Photo by Paul Conklin)

Emperor Haile Selassie and Sargent Shriver discussed the work of some 400 Peace Corps Volunteers in Ethiopia.

Mr. Shriver visited Peace Corps Volunteers in Turkey for a week early in 1964. Here (left) he is shown talking to a class of boys in the town of Akhisar, and (below) testing the English of two students of teacher Bill Aron of South Orange, New Jersey (with scarf).

(Photos by Paul Conklin)

At Nepalganj, on the border between Nepal and India, Mr. Shriver tried his hand at driving a tonga. (Below) He washed his face at a pump outside an agricultural school in southern Nepal, where he spent four days with Volunteers.

(Photos by Paul Conklin)

(Wide World Photos)

Sargent Shriver with President Johnson and Chancellor Ludwig Erhard (center), who is showing the President West Germany's pledge of $50,000 for the International Secretariat for Volunteer Service.

The Peace Corps Director confers with Dean Rusk, Secretary of State.

(Look *Magazine*)

nedy. The French Volunteers for Progress will be on their way to Africa before the end of the year. A new volunteer program for Great Britain, involving five hundred college graduates, has already begun. In Argentina, Belgium, New Zealand, Norway, Canada, and Australia, plans are being made to recruit, to train, and to send overseas additional volunteers.

This year over one thousand volunteers from other countries will be in the field. Next year we estimate the number will rise to more than 2,500. And the future knows no limit.

This is being done without costing the United States taxpayer a single cent. Every one of these Peace Corps will be financed, from start to finish, by the country which runs it. Three and a half million dollars has already been appropriated by foreign parliaments for this purpose. Next year more than ten million dollars will be earmarked by other countries for Peace Corps activities. All the United States has spent, over more than a year, is a contribution of less than $200,000 to help finance the Secretariat which has been instrumental in securing this multimillion-dollar effort by our free world allies. Nationals of five countries now work for the Secretariat, paid for by their own governments. Israel has supplied a full-time staff member to the Secretariat and was the first country to make a cash contribution. Other nations have already committed themselves to help support the work through cash contributions. The Netherlands has offered to supply, equip, and staff a European office for the organization.

We are on the verge of seeing the Peace Corps idea, the idea of voluntary service in the cause of human welfare, become the largest peaceful volunteer movement the world has ever seen.

All this is proof that the Peace Corps idea touches upon the profoundest needs of people throughout the world. Nowhere is this more dramatically illustrated than in the developing countries themselves. When we established the Secretariat, we thought it should also work to help establish volunteer groups run by the developing countries.

This idea too is moving ahead. The El Salvador Social Progress Corps is already in operation. Sixty Salvadoran volunteers are working alongside forty Americans in the villages and communities of El Salvador. In Africa a Secretariat member is working with the government of Northern Rhodesia; another is in Tanganyika, helping to prepare a domestic volunteer corps. The basic idea of these groups is to mobilize men and women to go out as volunteers to work in the schools and hospitals, farms and slums of their own countries. In other cases they will work on their own. The scale and skills, the form of the organization will differ from country to country. But the basic idea of volunteer service will remain the same. Thus the volunteer idea not only transcends national boundaries. It cuts across boundaries of wealth and poverty, race and religion, history and politics.

All this shows how right Albert Camus was when he said:

Great ideas come into the world as gently as doves. Perhaps, then, if we live attentively, we shall hear, amid the uproar of empires and nations, a faint flutter of wings—the gentle stirring of life and hope. Some will say that this hope lies in a nation; others, in a man. I believe rather that it is awakened, and revived, nourished by millions of solitary individuals whose deeds and works every day negate frontiers and the crudest implications of history. Each and every man, on the foundations of his own sufferings and joys, builds for all.

3. The Effect on American Society

California has produced more Peace Corps Volunteers than any other state in the Union. To report on their activities and to discuss the role they would play upon their return, Sargent Shriver in five days addressed twenty college convocations and meetings. This talk was to the Los Angeles World Affairs Council on October 7, 1963.

WE ARE, in the Peace Corps, involving people and institutions in the affairs of the world in a new, intimate, and dramatic way, a way which may well have far-reaching consequences for those individuals, for those institutions, for America and the world.

Let us take the private organizations of this country—ranging from the National Grange and YMCA to the Cooperative Association of America and savings and loan associations—the whole array of professional, occupational, and welfare groups which are the foundation of American life. When the Peace Corps began, a lot of people were afraid that we would not only discourage new organizations from getting into overseas work, but begin to edge out those who had done a good job over many years.

We were determined not to do this. We needed the private agencies to help us. And we hoped that we could be of some help to them. When we wanted to help develop cooperatives in Latin America, we went to the Cooperative Association of America for help. We are now working together on projects in eight different countries, and the cooperative movement is spreading rapidly throughout the hemisphere.

We found a great need for the kind of work the YMCA and YWCA were doing. Now we recruit, train, and ship people to work in their programs. As a result, the YWCA in Chile has five times the number of workers it did before the coming of the Peace Corps. The YMCA in Venezuela has increased four times.

The National Grange is the second largest farm organization in the country. It has four and a half million members. Yet it never had a program overseas. Today it is working with us in Guatemala, and we are exploring other ways in which the priceless know-how and experience of American farm organizations can be put to work in developing countries.

CARE is an organization that was overseas long before the Peace Corps was even a gleam in anyone's eye. Yet today they are working with the Peace Corps, administering some of our projects overseas, and sending men as well as material to the aid of the needy.

This is the opposite of big government and burgeoning bureaucracy. It is government and private enterprise working together, each helping the other to realize its own potential. It is evidence that through the Peace Corps we may have discovered a mechanism to bring the great resources of American private groups to bear on the needs and problems of the developing world, to turn them outward toward the problems of others as well as inward on their own problems. We are helping to provide a new dimension of work, of responsibility, and of rewards.

We would all agree that the quality of our educational system, its ability to train men and women for the rigors of the modern world, is one of the most significant problems in America today. I believe that in the future we may find the Peace Corps becoming one of the most significant shapers of the character of the nation's campuses—their response to, and their interest in, what is happening across the entire southern half of the globe.

Here is some of the evidence:

Recently President Virgil M. Hancher of the State University of Iowa wrote a letter to several Senators, discussing the training program which the university is running for Peace Corps Volunteers going to Indonesia. He said, in part:

The Peace Corps project is already having salutary effects upon this University. . . . The members of our faculty are having to come together across disciplines. They are having to think through old problems of education freshly and to tackle new ones. Along with the trainees they are learning—learning how to teach languages in the new method, how to teach new languages, how to teach area studies better. . . . The project is increasing the international dimension of the State University of Iowa. This international dimension is being shared, in various ways, with the people of the State, the Eastern area in particular.

Let me give you a concrete example of what President Hancher means, an example from my own home state of Illinois.

Northern Illinois University is in the heartland of America. It never had an international program. International affairs were not one of the top interests of the twenty thousand people who live in the neighboring town.

Working with the Peace Corps, Northern Illinois has trained three groups of Volunteers for Malaya. Here are some of the results: Six members of the Malayan Government have come there as teachers or lecturers. Northern Illinois is now one of the few places in the country teaching Malay, and five faculty members have visited Malaya. They have begun a Southeast Asia studies program, and the local newspaper now features news from that troubled area of the world. One of their faculty became the first director of the Peace Corps in Malaya.

And other schools are having the same sort of experience. More than fifty American universities, from Puerto Rico to Hawaii, have conducted programs to train Peace Corps Volunteers. More than two thousand faculty members have participated in these programs. And two hundred additional colleges have asked whether they too can participate.

In each of these universities, wherever a Peace Corps program is established, there is a surge of interest in a foreign land, an influx of eager and interested Volunteers, the arrival of groups of visiting instructors and foreign students who are brought to college for the training program. For a few months that college is an international center for studies of Thailand or Tanganyika, Malaya or Tunisia, or any one of almost fifty countries. This is an experience which leaves a mark on the life of the college and often, especially in rural areas, on the surrounding town.

We have already seen this happen with foreign language training. We have trained more people in more exotic languages than the entire National Defense Education Act. We have trained hundreds of Americans to speak Thai and Malay, Singhalese and Nepali, Twi, Kri, and Hausa—languages taught to not a single American under the NDEA. And in each case we have left behind on the campus new interest, new knowledge, sometimes even new dictionaries and textbooks opening up a fresh field of language studies for the college and, sometimes, for the country.

These are some of the results of the coming together of the Peace Corps and the colleges, the Volunteer and the professors, the government administrators and the college deans. It forecasts a Peace Corps influence on American education which will make it better able to meet its responsibilities to its students and the country.

Probably the most important development in the future of the Peace Corps will be the impact of returning Volunteers on American society. Before long five thousand Peace Corps Volunteers a year will be returning from having lived and worked overseas, under difficult conditions, among strange cultures, lands, and people. They will be a new breed of Americans, or rather the revival of an old breed of Americans—the Americans who believed everything was possible to the man of determination, the Americans who believed some things were more important than material affluence or personal success.

They will be coming back to teach in our schools, man posts in our government, work in our industries, participate in the affairs of nation and state, town and precinct. And from what I have seen of these men and women, none of the institutions to which they come will be secure behind a wall of complacency, indifference, or self-satisfaction.

The first several hundred Volunteers are already returning. They are a happy augury for the future. Let me tell you about some of them:

Cardozo High School is located in the midst of the worst slums of Washington, D.C., and the slums of Washington are bad and violence-ridden indeed. Last week ten former Peace Corps Volunteers, men and women who had taught in the barrios of the Philippines, began teaching the underprivileged students of Cardozo High. Each will teach two classes, and help to develop special programs for teaching the disadvantaged. They find in this job the same outlet for dedication and energy they first uncovered in the barrios of the Philippines.

"My Peace Corps service made me aware of the unity of man," said one. "It doesn't matter whether one is Filipino or American, we do the same things for the same reasons."

"I had planned to return to Alabama to teach," said another, "but the Cardozo project is so similar to the Peace Corps, so creative, that I had to join it."

And Cardozo is just an early tangible contribution of some of the more than 15 percent of returning Volunteers who want to make teaching their life's work.

Teaching, however, is only one of the beneficiaries. Fifty of the first 278 returnees will go to work in the Federal Government. Others will work in state and local governments. Many have already come to work in the Peace Corps; and I hope, in the not too distant future, that every office in the Peace Corps will be occupied by a returned Volunteer.

Nor is the Peace Corps the only agency to benefit. Returning Volunteers will go into the Foreign Service, USIA, into the AID programs and into other aspects of our overseas operations. I don't think that it is bragging to say that their work, their combination of idealism and concrete practicality, their experience with frustration and with satisfaction, will prove a new source of vigor and imagination to our bureaucracies.

Not all the returning Volunteers will go to work. Over half will continue their education, more than a third on special scholarships and fellowships. They have learned from their Peace Corps experience that knowledge and learning are needed to cope with the complexities of today's world. As a result, they will be more valuable citizens for the future, to say nothing of what their presence in classrooms will do to spur on and challenge teachers and other students alike.

Private industry will be another beneficiary of the returning Volunteer. If I were the personnel director of a major American company, I would look hopefully to the pool of returning Volunteers. They have been selected by a rigorous process from the cream of the nation's youth. They have survived a demanding training program. They have displayed qualities of high motivation, capacity to adjust, and skills which have enabled them to spend two successful years working with the people of a foreign country. All of this is becoming obvious to alert companies. More and more are asking for the chance to interview returning Volunteers. When Caterpillar Tractor trained some Volunteers for Tunisia, the head of training for the company told me, "There are six of those men we would like to hire right here." And they hadn't even gone overseas.

I believe that our Volunteers can be of real importance to American business as business becomes more and more involved in world trade, the opening up of new markets, and plant expansion overseas.

This is only a little of the evidence, the growing indications, of the effects that the returning Peace Corps Volunteer will have on American society. It is all we can talk about now. But there will be more. In two world wars Americans went overseas to fight and, when they returned, brought with them ideas and experiences which profoundly shaped the course of our history. Today Americans are going overseas not to fight but to work, not to resolve conflicts but to maintain peace, not to destroy tyranny but to build for freedom. They are the veterans of the sixties and the seventies. I hope, and I predict, that they will be the advance guard of the new America.

IV

THE WAR

ON

POVERTY

"The world is very different now. For man
holds in his mortal hands the power to abolish all
forms of human poverty and all forms of human life."
— JOHN F. KENNEDY, Inaugural Address

From the first hours of his administration, President Johnson
has been determined to organize a War on Poverty "because,"
as he said to Congress, "it is right, and because it is wise, and
because, for the first time in our history, it is possible to conquer poverty."

With the help of the Secretary of Labor, the Secretary of
Health, Education, and Welfare, the Secretary of Agriculture,
the Secretary of Defense, and the Chairman of the President's
Council of Economic Advisers, and of a special staff that worked
night and day for many weeks, we were able to prepare for
the President and present to Congress a program that not only
expanded earlier efforts but, as President Johnson said, "charts
a new course."

We all recognized that America has been engaged in a war
on poverty from the beginning. And we accepted the American
way of doing it, by opening new opportunities.

We also recognized that whatever we did would fit into the
larger picture of existing or already proposed policies for economic growth and welfare: the tax cut, Social Security, housing
programs, health care, minimum wages, area redevelopment,
manpower training, to name only a few. Our task was to provide a new focus on the hard-core poverty that these programs
have not reached, and to give the whole national effort new
thrust.

95

The resulting Economic Opportunity Act of 1964 includes new assistance to young people working their way through school, to unemployed young people lacking any employable skill, to small businessmen and small farmers. It provides three new institutions: a Job Corps, a Community Action Program, a corps of Volunteers in service to America.

These new programs alone will not solve the problem, any more than the Peace Corps could alone accomplish America's overseas aims. They are just the first steps. But like the Peace Corps, they should set a new pace and a new pattern, and serve as a catalyst for the national commitment and the further federal, state, and local action that will be necessary.

What is most important is that for the first time in history we are committing ourselves to a *war* on poverty. "This," said President Johnson in his message on poverty, "is a total commitment by this President, and this Congress, and this Nation, to pursue victory over the most ancient of mankind's enemies."

1. Myths That Mislead

The Advertising Council, meeting in Washington, D.C., on May 5, 1964, heard Sargent Shriver make this plea for a public information program.

LAST WEEK a famous woman journalist said to me, "Before you can do anything about poverty, you'll have to fumigate the closet in which Americans keep their ideas about the poor. You'll have to rid America of all its clichés about the poor, clichés like the one which says that only the lazy and worthless are poor, or that the poor are always with us."

She may be right. Our minds are so cluttered up with myths, slogans, and clichés about the poor that it would be a public service if you would help us clear the air.

Cliché Number One about the poor is based on a misinterpretation of the Bible. This myth maintains that the poor will always be with us. St. Matthew would rise up in justifiable distress if he knew how callous people used his words to justify their inaction and indifference toward the poor. Pope Pius XII spoke for every truly religious leader in modern times when he said that the consequences of poverty were "a dying daily, a dying hourly; a dying multiplied, especially for parents by the number of dear ones they behold suffering and wasting away." When the Pope said that every Christian "will be diligent to achieve the betterment of the poor and the disinherited," he was only echoing the thoughts of the Jewish prophets, the Hindu gurus, and the Moslem mullahs. What every religion says about the poor is that we must make them our personal concern, for, as the Bible reminds us, "He that giveth unto the poor shall not lack but he that hideth his eyes shall have many a curse."

Furthermore, this myth ignores the fact that modern technology has provided us, for the first time, with the possibility of wiping out physical poverty.

Cliché Number Two—that you can't make a silk purse out of a sow's ear—is nonsense. Du Pont spends millions each year to prove just the opposite, to demonstrate technology's ability to make better things through chemistry. A very serviceable silk purse *has* been made out of a sow's ear.

The poor do not enjoy poverty. They resent it. Where local communities have started programs to help the poor help themselves, the response has exceeded expectations. The poor do want to learn, they do want the equal opportunity to work, and they will work hard for their own improvement.

Myth Number Three—that American society will always have a second division; that you can't have the Yankees without the Senators or a first-place team without a last-place team —is more sophisticated. Of course, there will always be some segment of American population not so well off as the rest. But no one connected with the poverty program proposes to equalize life's burdens. Helping the poor help themselves is the keynote of the President's program. It does not offer handouts; it offers opportunities. It is concerned with creating the conditions under which the child born into poverty can have the chance to help himself, to compete on equal terms with those lucky enough to be born into affluence.

Slogan Number Four says, "Things are worse every place

else." Being poor in America becomes, by this kind of verbal hocus-pocus, a sort of lucky break. On the contrary, there is a special degradation of the spirit, a hopelessness, a sense of being outcast from society, that comes from poverty in the midst of affluence. Where the national average income of a country is only fifty dollars per year, the pain of exclusion does not bear so heavily on the family which has only forty dollars. But in America technology has provided all of us, poor and rich alike, with a vision of our abundance, of a world of new cars, ski slopes, and suburbs.

We can win the War Against Poverty because we have the tools, we have the know-how, and we have the will. In the face of that combination, even the strongest myths will melt away.

A key tool in the program is the Job Corps, made up of 100,000 young volunteers from the approximately one million now between the ages of sixteen and twenty-one who are both out of school and out of work. The Job Corps will give these volunteers an opportunity over a two-year period to acquire the skills they will need to get, and to keep, their first job. It means getting them, for the first time in their lives, out of the poverty-blighted neighborhoods in which they roam today, jobless, rootless, and potentially dangerous.

The War on Poverty proposes to create 200,000 community jobs for jobless youths and 145,000 school-related jobs. The latter will let youngsters stay in school and college who would otherwise have to drop out and deprive us all of their potential contribution to society.

This war means creating and encouraging hundreds of community action plans in the places where poverty is concentrated. It means, as well, loans and grants to potential businessmen—self-employers, really—to get started or continue where no normal credit channels are open. It means small cash grants to willing farmers and farm families, who can get the capital they need in no other way, thus enabling them to stay on the farms they like instead of migrating to big-city relief rolls.

Poverty has as many different faces as the different places where it is found. What will work in Cleveland may not work in Los Angeles, and a program which Chicago might use to fight urban slum poverty will not take root in the rocky soil of Appalachia. That is why the heart of the poverty legislation is *local* community action and *voluntary* participation. There will be no poverty czars; there will be no great bureaucracy. But there will be federal assistance for local plans, worked out and presented by local leaders.

Will these programs work? A better question might be: What is working now?

Local community action programs already exist in many centers of poverty, and numerous communities have already prepared plans and await only the signal to go ahead.

Once there was a theory that IQ's were fixed at birth; today educators have proved this wrong and demonstrated that the potential of intelligence is related directly to poverty.

In St. Paul, Minnesota, a remedial program at the high school with the highest dropout rate in the city succeeded in cutting that rate down to the second lowest in only five years. Here, too, the relationship between school dropout rates and poverty was unmistakable.

In Chicago, Illinois, a basic job training program offered to long-term unemployed parents has had dramatic results. Thirty-two thousand people were able to get off the Cook County relief rolls because of this program. Today these people are driving taxis, working in hotels, restaurants, hospitals, and filling stations. Even more important, they have taken the first step toward full citizenship: they have a job.

In New Haven, Connecticut, community action programs involve preschools, adult literacy classes, homemaking and job-training centers, and, in addition, the program established neighborhood legal aid clinics. Here the poor, many for the first time, can get desperately needed legal advice on everything from a juvenile arrest to a conditional sales contract. More than a million young people under twenty-one have some kind of arrest record. Many of them are unemployable today because of bad or nonexistent legal help. And even worse, we live in a society where crime in the central city becomes just juvenile high spirits out in the suburbs. It is a sober fact that it is only delinquent children with families who can be turned over to their families. For the others, the children of poverty, the only alternative to an overworked police force is the juvenile hall.

The Chicago Adult Education Program will not fit every poverty-ridden urban center. Perhaps the New Haven Legal Aid Clinic is not needed in your community. The program President Johnson has presented to the Congress clearly represents an understanding that each community must solve its problems in its own way and under its own leadership. With assistance from the government, programs such as these can expand and grow; new and imaginative ones can be created. The problem of poverty in America demands action at all levels.

There has been some legitimate criticism directed toward the program. It is not broad enough, some critics say. I agree. It does not have enough funds, others point out. I agree. And there are those who say it is not correct to describe it as a war. They may be right.

Yet what is being proposed in the program is one necessary step toward the elimination of poverty. The tax cut was another. No one in the administration believes that the tax cut alone or the poverty program alone or the Appalachia program alone will win the war on poverty. But we know that together all these programs will at least take us on the next step of our journey.

2. Why We Can Win

This argument against a Gallup Poll report was addressed to the final dinner of the American Society of Newspaper Editors, meeting in Washington on April 18, 1964.

MANY AMERICANS do not share President Kennedy's conviction that now "man holds in his mortal hands the power to abolish all forms of human poverty. . . ." Three weeks ago, the Gallup Poll reported that 83 percent of the American people do not believe we can win the war against poverty. They are wrong.

Henrik Ibsen maintained that "The minority is always in the right." When I look at the Gallup Presidential Poll I can't agree with Ibsen. But when it comes to the War Against Poverty I know that the majority is not well informed about the ability we now have to eliminate poverty. I am here tonight to solicit your help, therefore, in one of the most important information programs our country has ever needed. For if you and your readers are given the facts accurately, I believe you will agree that this is one of the great news stories of our time.

Suppose you had been in Baltimore in 1893, about the time when the first modern medical school in America was established at Johns Hopkins University. Suppose you had had the privilege of attending a dinner like this and of hearing from Dr. Welch, or Dr. Halsted, or Dr. Osler. Any one of them could have told you that night in 1893 that medicine was on the verge of great new breakthroughs for the benefit of mankind. They could have pictured for you the elimination of all infectious disease. They could have predicted that modern medicine and public health practices would eliminate the ancient scourges of mankind, like rickets and scurvy.

Today we know that the revolution in medicine, bringing with it an extraordinary increase in man's life expectancy, is one of the great revolutions of the twentieth century, a revolution which has not yet expended its force, a revolution which has played a crucial role in bringing about the population explosion.

Or suppose you had been sitting at Franklin Delano Roosevelt's right hand when he opened the historic letter from Albert Einstein telling the President that in Einstein's judgment it was technically possible to split the atom.

Both of these incidents were news stories of transcendent importance. But both of them would have been rejected as fantasy by at least 83 percent of the American people if they had been interviewed in a Gallup Poll at that time.

Today we are at another watershed in the history of mankind. For despite the doubts of the people, it is, as President Kennedy stated, now possible, certainly within our nation, to eliminate all forms of human poverty.

This unprecedented possibility did not exist fifty years ago. No nation at that time had the essential ingredients for success. But today we in America do possess those ingredients:

First, we have the wealth to win. In material and human resources this nation is unequaled. With a Gross National Product already greater than $600 billion per annum, we could eliminate all economic poverty in the U.S.A. tomorrow, simply by giving income supplements of $11 billion to all the poor. No one suggests that. But it proves how easy it would be—less than 2 percent of our Gross National Product—to do the job. That is how strong we are, how vast our wealth.

Put another and better way, if we could raise the income of

the poor families in America just $1,000 per annum per family, we would raise our Gross National Product $14 billion and create additional consumer purchasing power equal to the combined markets of Oregon, Oklahoma, and Colorado.

We cannot afford to deny ourselves the benefits of a program capable of accomplishing such results. Every single item in the President's war on poverty aims at these objectives, and every one of the proposals pays for itself.

Less than $5,000 invested in a Job Corps youth can raise his lifetime earnings by at least $60,000.

A one-time grant of $1,500 invested in a farm family can keep it from migrating to the city where welfare payments would cost this much in less than six months.

For $300 to $500, the head of a family on welfare can be trained for a job, a cost which is offset if his time on relief is reduced by only two or three months.

These are only a few examples of our national capacity in productivity and income to win the War Against Poverty.

Second, we have the knowledge of economics and the fiscal and monetary tools and techniques to win.

It's easy to forget how new the Federal Reserve System really is with its sophisticated controls over the money supply, how new are the SEC, FTC, the Council of Economic Advisers to the President, the Social Security System, the minimum wage laws, and full employment policies incorporated in the Act of 1946. Yet these are all essential forces available to us.

Moreover, in the last three years we have witnessed an extraordinary new acceptance of advanced economic theories by the Congress. The recent tax cut passed in a period of economic growth indicates Congressional acceptance of the fact that government can and should accelerate the expansion of our economy even in periods of relative prosperity. The new provisions for more liberal depreciation allowances, the interest equalization tax, the subtle techniques of credit control which maintain low interest rates at home with high rates abroad are additional examples.

How many of you know that the Treasury and the Federal Reserve have been dancing their own version of the twist since 1961? Chubby Checkers has not been playing the music, but the Treasury Twist has checked, for the first time in history, the harmful fluctuations in the short- and long-term rates always connected with economic expansion in the past. The Treasury Twist, in fact, has kept the short-term interest rate up and the long-term interest rate down—a feat never before accomplished during a period of broad economic growth.

Even in the international monetary field we have witnessed an unprecedented development. Close collaboration between the central banks of European countries and our own Treasury has prevented speculation in gold. Thus we have protected our economic flank as we forge ahead internally with the expansion of our own economy. And the new wage-price guideposts hold out the promise of price stability over long periods of growth.

Most of this is new since 1946; all of it is new in the last fifty years. Combined with large-scale public investment in the education, training, and social development of human beings, we can create an ever-expanding economy.

For those who still believe these policies are not effective, I suggest they talk to General Motors, A. T. & T., and American Electric Light and Power. These companies in the last few weeks have announced six billion dollars in capital expansion, based in large part on their optimistic evaluation of the economic growth potential of our country operating under the policies outlined above.

Third, we have the new educational training techniques to win.

In the last five years, a special program in New York City raised the IQ's of fifty thousand children in grades three through ten by an average of 13 points and some by 20 points. Recently in Illinois Dr. Samuel Kirk raised the IQ's of eighty four-year-old mentally retarded children from 72 to 89 just by giving them intensive, special instruction one hour a day, five days a week, for a year. Never has so dramatic a change in IQ been achieved so rapidly. His proven techniques with such young, and even mentally retarded, children open a new panorama of opportunity for normal but culturally deprived children.

There are other programs for children where IQ's of 60 have been raised to IQ's of 95. This may not mean much to you; hardly anyone gets to be an editor with an IQ of 95. But that difference between 60 and 95 is the difference between a helpless, almost useless being, a burden on society, a "tax-eater," and a useful citizen, able to earn a living, read a newspaper, and buy the things it advertises.

Not long ago, Professor Zacharias of MIT visited our office and said, "For ten years I have been helping the military learn how to kill people cheap. I intend to spend the next ten years learning how to teach people cheap." His special Committee on Educational Research and Development has already produced its first paper on how to create first-class education for the masses in our slums. It is an optimistic paper, full of new ways to wage the War on Poverty by helping to educate our children and youth better.

Fourth, we have the means of communication and the mobility of population to win.

Henry Ford made America a nation on wheels. But even he could not have foreseen the unprecedented mobility of our population between states, within states, and even within cities.

In Chicago when I served on the Board of Education, thousands of children shifted schools three, four, even five times a year as their parents moved about seeking better work, better housing, or better schools. And in our War Against Poverty we shall use the Job Corps not only to change attitudes and create skills, but to help the poor get where the going is good. Americans today do *not* have to remain in a pocket of poverty.

G. K. Chesterton once said, "The Russians eliminate pickpockets by eliminating pockets." We'll do them one better. We shall eliminate pockets of poverty without eliminating the pocket-dwellers. We shall do this—with your help—with information campaigns, with education, through the Job Corps, through job training, and with incentives for study.

Finally, we can win because for the first time in history we have the will to win.

The Soviet Union talks about competition. They claim their system can do more to advance the welfare of people than ours, that Communism can alone meet the needs of the poor. If it is peaceful competition they want, we are ready to compete. We challenge Khrushchev to a race, not a race to see who can build bigger bombs or field larger armies, but a race to see who can first build a society without poverty, a society in which no one is underprivileged, in which all have the full rewards of their ability. Let him join us in a declaration of war against poverty. And we will show who can win that war.

We will win because our poverty program does not rely exclusively on big government, on big business, or on big labor. Happily, we do have the support of the leaders in these three crucial groups. But more important, we have the support of those American people who actually know what the battle is all about.

More than ten thousand letters endorsing our efforts have already arrived at our headquarters. Governors, mayors, economists, and educators have testified for the program. Even one of Senator Goldwater's economists, Raymond J. Saulnier, endorses our part of the attack on unemployment when he writes, ". . . that residual unemployment in our economy is due mainly to lack of skills, inadequate educational backgrounds, unsuitable or inadequate work experience, and discrimination." And twenty business, education, and labor executives are already working, without compensation, at our temporary headquarters.

This is not a program which proposes a quick and easy solution to poverty, nor is it the beginning or the end of the War on Poverty. It is part of a coordinated attack on poverty, the first one in our history with a real chance to win.

This program is workable. It relies on local initiative. It calls for personal participation by individual Americans. It encourages the American free, private enterprise system. And it is voluntary. Philosophically it is in tune with our highest ideals.

The United States of America was not founded just so more people could get rich, but for ideals: the ideals of equality among men, of liberty for all, of religious and political freedom for the individual.

This spirit was well summed up by a great artist and man, Pablo Casals, the Spanish cellist now living in Puerto Rico. Two years ago, he spoke to a meeting attended by delegates from forty-three nations gathered together to discuss the Peace Corps. Casals talked about the Peace Corps, but what he said applies with equal force to the President's program against poverty. Here is what he said:

"This is new and it is also very old. We have in a sense come full circle. We have come from the tyranny of the enormous, awesome, discordant machine back to a realization that the beginning and end are man, that it is man who is important, not the machine, that it is man who accounts for growth, not just dollars or factories, and above all that it is man who is the object of all our efforts."

3. Who Is Responsible for the Poor?

These remarks were prepared for but never delivered at the Georgetown University commencement exercises on June 8, 1964. Just as Mr. Shriver started to talk, a heavy thunderstorm intervened. Excerpts from the talk were published in America *Magazine, with whose permission they are reprinted here.*

SOON THREE THOUSAND of our first Peace Corps Volunteers will be home. They have learned about the world, not in an abstract way, not in books, but in service—in service of the poor; the poor in education, the poor in health, the poor in spirit. They have learned how to serve. They have learned responsibility.

They are coming home feeling responsible for their own country. They now feel responsible for poverty in America. But why should they? Why should you? Why should I? Who is really responsible for the poor?

Is Georgetown University responsible, even for the poor of the nation's capital, the community in which the university was born and has grown to international eminence? Its primary responsibility is surely to its students and to the educational process. Our academic gowns remind us of the high educational purposes of the university. Is it fair to ask it to distract itself from these purposes?

Is this faculty responsible for the poor? Surely, the task of educating young men and women should be practically all-consuming. Are the students of this university responsible? What time do they have to spare when they should devote themselves fully to their studies, to the academic excellence this nation needs and this school must require?

How responsible for the poor can you be while embarking on commendable pursuits and professions? A lawyer's first responsibility is to his client. A doctor's is to his patient. A businessman's duty is to make profits for his stockholders, his partners, his family.

So, then, who is responsible for the poor?

That leaves only the poor themselves. But they can't all be responsible for their poverty. One-third of today's poor are children. Can anyone claim they got to be poor because they are lazy, shiftless, drunken, or profligate? They were born poor. And most of their parents were born into poverty. You will find millions of American children who are the third or fourth generation of poverty in their families. We cannot hold these children responsible.

Many of the poor are Negroes. They are born with a legacy worse than just poverty. They are born with the mark of slavery and discrimination, with skin that for five generations has shut doors to them. A Negro cannot be held responsible for the color that God gave him.

You can point to me and say, "President Johnson made you responsible." But that makes me feel like Mrs. Astor on the sinking ship *Titanic*. As the iceberg crashed through the ship's walls, she said, "I asked for ice, but this is ridiculous."

Poverty is like an iceberg. Although submerged, cold, and impersonal, it can crash into our lives. When a professor is attacked on a city street, when a gang holds up a subway car, when a bystander is killed in a riot, when little girls are bombed in a church, we suddenly feel one cutting edge of poverty.

Poverty is like an iceberg because it chills us, it freezes our hearts, it makes us cold and impersonal. It is so frightening that we turn our eyes away from the human constituents of poverty, the people who are drowning in the sea of poverty—the men without jobs, the mothers without a man, or money, the children on the streets. These are the ones who feel the sharpest edge of poverty.

The worst news story of the year was about the murder of a woman in New York who could have been saved by onlookers. But not one of thirty-eight witnesses came to her aid, not one raised a hand, not one even uttered a cry or called the police until it was all over. No one was ready to go out into the night! No one felt responsible! When we reach this pit, this bottom, there can be no way but up. This kind of irresponsibility is the great pitfall of our complex, modern civilization.

The way up is not easy. But if any graduating class should know it, if any university should teach it, it should be here. For among the books you read, among the words you ponder, are some ancient ones: "For what is a man profited, if he gain the whole world, and lose his own soul?"

For what will it profit you or me if we reach the height of our professions, and we find ourselves indifferent and our lives narrow? For what will it profit this university if, after all its good education, it graduates its students into irresponsibility?

I wonder what kind of education the Good Samaritan had. I suspect that those who passed by that miserable man who had been thrown among robbers probably had college degrees. Certainly they were busy with their professions—too busy to take responsibility for someone who was dirty, half naked, and half dead.

We all raise shields against the poor. Then we say that poverty is invisible. What President Johnson is asking us to do is very simple, but very hard: he is asking us to lower these shields. He is confident that once we see what needs to be done, we will do it.

The President's task force on the War Against Poverty is

going to do its part. Are you going to do your part? Are you who are graduating today going to graduate into responsibility? Are you who stay on to study and to teach in the years to come going to practice responsibility right here at Georgetown? Or are you going to turn your back on the hungry and the poor and the strangers on our streets here in Washington?

If you on the faculty tell your students that their only responsibility is to their academic studies, if you tell them to think of themselves solely as students, then you are laying the pattern for a lifetime of irresponsibility. If today students are taught to use their books as shields, tomorrow they will find their professions or their family obligations just as effective shields. That is what I mean by graduating students into irresponsibility.

You might say that I am wrong here, that the student of today will join the Peace Corps tomorrow. I hope so, for that is one way to put down your shields and serve your fellow man, full time, for a short period of your life. And when you come back home, you could join the War on Poverty.

But do we need this period of service abroad to learn how to serve at home? If we do, then we are in real trouble. Because the Peace Corps barely scratches the surface of our needs. Soon there will be ten thousand Peace Corps Volunteers. But there are half a million college graduates this year alone. There are over two million college and university students in our land. If ten thousand are to learn responsibility in the Peace Corps, and two million are to practice the irresponsibility of their specializations, then we are in deep trouble. If we don't commit ourselves to waging the War on Poverty, if you in our universities and student bodies and faculties don't commit yourselves to this, then the iceberg of poverty is going to bring real havoc to our cities, to our backdoors, yes, even to this university campus.

You of Georgetown have already taken a significant step in this direction. That is, three hundred of your students and faculty members have started on the road to responsibility. They volunteered to give their time, to give some time each week, to serve in twenty-four different social action projects in this city.

From an office under the staircase in Healey lobby, they go out to work in slum neighborhoods and schools. They go out to work with the children of the slums—those behind in school and those out of school and out of work. They do special tutoring, organize sports programs, assist in community organizations, serve in understaffed hospitals and settlement houses. They work Saturdays, on weekday afternoons, and throughout the summer vacation. They are learning the hard way, but the real way, who the poor are, and what poverty means. For them statistics take on faces. The sixty thousand faceless, functional illiterates of Washington have become people to them— boys and girls they are teaching to read. Poverty for them has become something personal.

Is this all a distraction from their true work as students? Far from subverting the educational process, this program is helping to fulfill it. In accepting responsibility for poverty, and for the great social problems of our national life, these three hundred Georgetown volunteers are pointing the way to a new frontier in American education: the Frontier of Service.

By serving in this way these men and women will not only be better Americans; they will be better doctors, better lawyers, better businessmen, better Foreign Service officers. The very nature of a profession is service. But when do students learn this most essential part? Medical students are too busy with intensive studies in medical school. A course in professional legal responsibility is usually offered in the law school curriculum, but not required. But what can be conveyed there about a lawyer's or a doctor's duty to the poor compared with what these Georgetown volunteers are experiencing? These volunteers are learning the compassion without which no profession or person is complete, the compassion that keeps us from by-passing the poor.

Take Jules Clavadetcher, a Georgetown student who all this year worked five hours a week at All Souls' Unitarian Church with some hostile and potentially delinquent Negro children. So marked was the good effect upon the children that the Jewish women's organization of B'nai B'rith awarded this Catholic student its yearly citation for enlightened civic action for youth. Jules learned a lot about the problems of race and poverty. Maybe he learned something about the Ecumenical movement, too.

The chairman of your own Philosophy Department, Dr. Jesse Mann, tells me, "I would much rather have students in my class of Philosophy 104 learning about the philosophy of man by working with underprivileged Negro children of this city than merely by reading dusty volumes in Riggs Library."

So these students who are passing up a beer party or a dance or a lazy Saturday afternoon in favor of this work are not subverting Georgetown. This program of university service is rather the extension of education, the broadening of education, the deepening of education which we must have if we are to find our way through the web of modern technology, through our technical specialties into our full responsibilities as human beings.

Fortunately, the needs of American education and the needs of our War on Poverty meet at this point. For what you have begun here is what we must launch on a vast scale, if we are to win the War on Poverty.

All of American higher education should respond, but there is a special call to all those colleges and universities which like Georgetown stand in the shadow of the Cross. For this war against poverty is America's Holy War. And if you fail to respond, you will deeply wrong yourselves, your country, and your faith.

In our great sacraments, we see the love of God for man. Because His word became flesh, we vow to try to make the word become flesh in our own inadequate lives. There is another "sacrament" that can help us learn how to do this, a "sacrament" that can give us the strength to keep on trying to do it. It is the "Sacrament of Service to Man-in-Need."

Christ considered this so important that He made our final judgment turn, not on the number of prayers we say, but on whether or not we are too busy to help Him when He comes to us in the garments of the poor. "I was hungry, and you gave me to eat: I was thirsty, and you gave me to drink: I was a stranger, and you took me in . . . as long as you did it to one of these my least brethren, you did it to me."

So it is time, as it has always been time, for us to lower our shields, and to see the sacrament awaiting us beyond the altar rail, outside the campus gates. It is this mission to which we are sent, when we leave the chapel that stands at the heart of this campus. "*Ite missa est*" does not mean our trivial translation, "It is finished, you can go." It means, instead, "Go and fulfill your mission."

4. The Politics of Service

This address was delivered at the June 10, 1964, commencement exercises of New York University. As Sargent Shriver began speaking, the vote on cloture for the Civil Rights Bill was being taken in the United State Senate and before he concluded, a message was handed him saying that for the first time in history cloture had been imposed on a civil rights debate. Mr. Shriver cited this vote as a result of the kind of "politics of service" he was advocating.

POLITICS in its full sense goes far beyond primaries or even general elections. The root of the word politics is *polis*, the Greek word for the city, or city-state. A politician in ancient times was supposed to serve the city. And serving the city in that ancient sense includes serving the nation and even mankind today. That is the kind of politics we need now—*the politics of service.*

Mahatma Gandhi demonstrated this kind of politics in India. He chose to live and work among the poor. He always rode the third-class trains with the poor, he said, because there was no fourth class. At first, people laughed at him when he called on the Indian people to vote for independence with their feet, by joining him in his famous Salt March to the sea. But this politics of deeds, not words, achieved the independence of one-sixth of the human race.

The politics of service is also a creative kind of politics. It built the State of Israel, farm by farm, *kibbutz* by *kibbutz*, town by town. Those pioneers in Palestine, working with their hands, started little islands of the twentieth century that turned Death Valleys into green gardens.

The American labor movement understands this politics of service. Millions of men and women have "voted" for unions with their feet—on the picket lines. And then they have gone on to create, with their own resources, union programs of health care, education, and cooperative housing.

Martin Luther King, Jr., rose on the American scene like a star in the night when he led thousands of Americans in the Montgomery bus boycott. They were "voting" for full human rights with their feet. An old woman who walked miles to work rather than be segregated on a bus was asked by a newspaper-man if she wasn't tired. "My feet are tired," she said, "but my soul is resting."

The students who are volunteering this summer to register voters in areas where this takes great courage, the men and women of the NAACP and the National Urban League, and other civil rights organizations, who have struggled long and courageously, all know the power that comes from this kind of politics. They know how tired the feet can get, but how satisfying this is to the soul.

The secret of the Peace Corps' success is this same politics of service. Peace Corps service is a practical way to convert our ideas into action. Our Volunteers have been "voting" for peace with their feet, their hands, their heads, and their hearts. They are out in the world serving the larger city we now live in, the City of Man. For Peace Corps Volunteers that city of the world has become a real community. They have learned how much people everywhere have in common across the barriers of color and language and culture. Volunteers have learned foreign languages, but most of all they have learned to hear the voice of the human heart in any language.

During their two years in foreign lands, the Volunteers did not lose touch with America. Instead, they discovered how closely America and the rest of the world have become linked. But they will not be the same men and women who left. Here is what one Volunteer in Ethiopia wrote to his parents recently: "I have changed, and those who came with me have changed. Whatever we were before, and none of us can quite remember, that's all gone." Dick Lipez adds: "Peace Corps life tempers one by its sheer and irresistible intensity." "We look forward to coming home," he wrote, "but 'missing' will be the adventure, the thrill that none of us will ever be able to live again with such intensity, such freedom." In meeting their responsibilities of service, he said, "We found a kind of freedom greater than any we could have imagined."

But why should this kind of freedom, the freedom that comes from service, be missing in our lives at home? Is it true that it can only come in serving the larger City of the World, and not in serving the City of New York? The people who are going to wage war on poverty are not in Washington. They are already living on the front lines of poverty, right in the centers of our cities. I call upon the faculty and student body of New York University and of all other great universities to practice the politics of service here at home in your own neighborhoods— not by more courses in responsibility or in American social problems, not by lectures, not by commencement talks; but by political action in this true sense of politics, in the service of your city.

Is this too much to ask of this university, to suggest that you take the blocks around you, that you take this city, as your laboratory, that you do your research in the service of the people you live among, that you make community action programs to end poverty in New York a focus of your study and the center of your extracurricular activities?

Remember what this university was founded for 133 years ago: to be a school in which "the children of the artisan and the tradesman should be as welcome as the children of the rich." But you are all rich—rich in education, the key to the twentieth century—or you wouldn't be here today. The poor for whom this university was founded are out in the night, in the streets, in the overcrowded schools needing extra teachers, in the hospitals needing extra help, in the settlement houses needing volunteers. They need your help. We need your help. We need men and women who will work in these programs and start new programs of their own. For this we need the manpower and the brainpower, we need the service of the colleges and universities of America.

Peace Corps Volunteers by the thousands are now coming home. For them poverty is not invisible. They have lived in it; they have worked with people in other parts of the world to eliminate it. They will see it in America, and they will see no excuse for it. They will be right. And they will do their part. In a poll of the first returning Volunteers, four out of five said they were interested in working to end poverty at home, and 30 percent said they were ready to volunteer, part time or full time, right away. A Peace Corps Volunteer, a white boy from Alabama, last week volunteered to teach in an all-Negro slum in Washington, D.C.

But the returning Peace Corps Volunteers are not the answer. American higher education, two million strong, must carry the main load. There are half a million college graduates this year alone. What about them? What kind of blood runs in their veins? Are they learning to serve? With nearly fifty thousand students and faculty, this university alone overshadows the whole Peace Corps in its resources and potential power. What about you? Are you ready to practice the politics of service?

This is the new frontier required of American higher education. Once the education of man took place in ivory towers far from the scene of action. But this university, like modern man, has no such escape.

When America faced the unprecedented problem of splitting the atom, it turned to the American academic community, to some of our great universities. Einstein knew more than anyone else, yet even Einstein could only say that it could be done.

So the Manhattan Project tried something new in our public life. With no time to waste, it experimented with several approaches simultaneously. It took two main routes, one the plutonium route, one the route of uranium, U-235, and it tried variations on each. And as the major laboratory investigator of each approach it contracted with a major university. The University of Chicago worked on plutonium. Berkeley worked on separating the uranium isotope through the electromagnetic approach, using the cyclotron. Columbia worked on splitting uranium through another method, gaseous diffusion. Columbia also worked, with Princeton, on the centrifuge approach that didn't work and was dropped. Fifteen or twenty other universities played key parts.

We all know the results. The first chain reaction took place at Stagg Field at the University of Chicago on December 2, 1942. The first nuclear reaction took place at Alamogordo, New Mexico, on July 16, 1945. These events, the product of the service of American universities in time of war, changed the world.

Now we are engaged in a peacetime struggle, but one that is also a matter of life and death for our cities, and for millions of our people. In the War on Poverty there is no time to waste. That is why we must turn to our universities again. That is why we must ask for your total commitment. An all-university project to end the cycle of poverty in the areas where you live and have your being is within the intellectual and spiritual power of this, the largest private educational institution in the world.

If you do this and do it with all the resources at your command, then future generations will say that the problem of poverty was cracked, and that a chain reaction of progress was started here on University Heights and on Washington Square.

V

CIVIL

RIGHTS

"We shall be as a city upon a hill, and the eyes of all people are upon us."
— JOHN WINTHROP, Sermon to the Puritans in Mid-Atlantic, 1630

In the City of Chicago, as in America as a whole, much remains to be done before we are a city where equal opportunity is secured for all. The President's Economic Opportunity program is a vital part of what must be done, as the first two of the following talks emphasize. The other talks go back to 1958, when the Civil Rights Commission was just beginning its studies of discrimination in both the South and the North, and bringing to national attention the problem of *de facto* segregation. But several years before that I remember introducing to a Chicago audience a young minister in his twenties, Martin Luther King, Jr., who was then leading a bus boycott in Montgomery, Alabama. His subject was: "We've come a long, long way—but we've got a long, long way to go." That is still the right theme in discussing the greatest single moral issue before the nation.

1. A City upon a Hill

*This address to the National Convention of the National
Association for the Advancement of Colored People was given
on June 24, 1964, while the nation was concerned about the
three missing civil rights workers whose burned car had just
been found in a Mississippi swamp.*

IF SENATOR GOLDWATER really wants to find the Mainstream,
he should come here to this convention. He should come here
and explain why he thinks it unconstitutional to pass a law
guaranteeing equal opportunity for all Americans. At the
same time, he might try to explain his doctrine of states' rights.
He might explain how it has been working in Mississippi the
last two or three days.

Yet despite Senator Goldwater, the Civil Rights Bill is about
to become a landmark in American history. For this we owe
deep thanks to John Kennedy and Lyndon Johnson. But let
us never forget that the NAACP was in the fight for fifty years,
not fifty weeks, giving enduring and dedicated leadership. All
Americans, of all races and colors and creeds, owe you a great
debt of gratitude.

Somebody said that with this Civil Rights Bill our government is finally about to run on all three of its engines—not
only the Executive and the Judiciary, but finally the Legislative

engine. But do not forget the fourth engine, the power of the people.

You represent the power of the people—the power of the people to bring laws into existence and get them enforced. For fifty years, in times and places of danger as well as indifference, you spoke up for, you stood up for, you sat down for, you marched for, you picketed for, you protested and petitioned and sued for the basic rights of all Americans. You have done this in every forum and in every state. The Civil Rights Bill therefore is truly your latest victory, but it will not be your last.

For people like you the job is never done. Work goes on, and you must go on. We must go on together to give full reality to the great promises contained in the long line of laws designed to advance all the people of America—from the Bill of Rights itself, through the Thirteenth, Fourteenth, and Fifteenth Amendments, through the abolition of the poll tax, and the civil rights legislation of the last decade.

The latest of the laws to require your help and your support is the law which will enable us to start President Johnson's War Against Poverty.

In 1960, John Kennedy put these facts before us:

The Negro baby born in America today, regardless of the section of the nation in which he is born, has about one-half as much chance of completing high school as a white baby born in the same place on the same day, one-third as much chance of completing college, one-third as much chance of becoming a professional man, twice as much chance of becoming unemployed, about one-seventh as much chance of earning $10,000 a year, a life expectancy which is seven years shorter, and the prospect of earning only half as much.

The three significant aspects of the Negro Revolution found in these facts—employment, education, and health—are just as important today as in 1960, for that Negro baby of 1960 is now three and a half years old, with these odds still stacked against him. President Johnson's War on Poverty attacks each one of these problems.

First, it attacks the problem of jobs. The legal rights obtained in large part through the efforts of the NAACP will be empty promises without economic opportunities. The necessity for jobs was summed up eloquently by a young Negro woman on a national broadcast who was asked recently what her highest ambition in life was. She replied simply, "To marry a man with a job."

Something is wrong with a society where a young woman assumes that her husband normally would not have a job. How can we expect young men or women to prepare diligently for the skill or work required in an age of automation when they have been conditioned by doubt and by despair to expect no jobs, when they have seen their fathers out of work or restricted to dead-end jobs? Even today, although unemployment in our country has gone down to 4.4 percent, it is still 9 percent for Negro Americans. Through the Job Corps and through work-training and work-study programs we intend to provide new job opportunities.

The second important part of President Johnson's program is education. Eighty percent of our white people have completed grammar school, while only 50 percent of our Negro people have. Forty-one percent of our white people have completed high school, while only 16 percent of our Negro people have.

Through the "Community Action" part of the President's program, we will make it possible for school districts to start special nursery schools. These will help children, especially from minority groups, to do better in grammar school and to go on to high school. Communities will also start remedial reading clinics for those who cannot either get or hold a job because of faulty reading. There will be special summer schools, and adult

education, offered after school hours and at nighttime, in the
wintertime and in the summertime, so that older people can
get better jobs. There will be schools for parents, so that the
parents will have a better understanding of their responsibilities. There is also a work-study program to help hundreds of
thousands of young Americans today who could and should go
to college if they could finance their way.

Health is the third key factor. Remember the familiar cartoon
of a peasant sleeping under a tree with a sombrero over his
face. The myth is that the poor, especially the minority group
poor, don't want to work, that they are lazy or shiftless. Let me
say I have seen lazy and shiftless people of all races, colors,
and creeds all over the world. Race has got nothing to do
with it. What you get to eat has a lot more to do with it.
I have seen thousands of children with little swollen bellies.
You would think they had a lot to eat, but if they had anything to eat, all they had was starch. There are millions of
people who have had diseases from the time they were born.
They have had malaria, not once, but two or three times;
they have had beriberi, or scurvy, or rickets. When people say,
"Look at that lazy fellow; he doesn't want to work," I would
rather look at his blood stream and see how many diseases he
has had because of poor medical care.

With the help of communities across the country we can do
something about this. We can provide better prenatal service
for mothers. My wife and I recently computed that we spend
in the United States today more money on research and care of
pregnant cows than we do for pregnant women. Now we are
just beginning to find out that the prenatal care a woman gets
and the kind of care that she should give to her child between
birth and three years of age are as important as anything she
ever does for this child. This will control, in many respects, the
kind of life that child will lead. If his mother has poor nutrition
while carrying him, and if that child has poor nutrition and

poor care after birth, that child does not have an equal chance.

There are many other parts of President Johnson's poverty program. But we cannot help today focusing our thoughts on another kind of poverty. For what is happening in Mississippi, what is happening to those three young men, is poverty—the poverty of American law, power, and spirit. The picture of that burned car in Bogue Chitto swamp shows the world how poor we are.

This is the kind of poverty you have been working so long to eliminate. This is the kind of poverty the Civil Rights Bill, now before Congress, is designed to eliminate. And let me add that this is the kind of poverty which eight thousand Peace Corps Volunteers are working to eliminate all around the world. When they read the news of violence in America done to young volunteers like themselves, who were working to advance human rights at home, they will see, they will feel, how poor America is.

We have sent Volunteers to more than three thousand different locations in forty-six different nations all over the world. They work with alien people, people full of suspicion of outsiders, and distrust of the West, distrust of the United States. But in three years we have not had a single incident of violence to a Peace Corps Volunteer serving abroad. We have heard a lot of talk about backward people on other continents. But when we think of that burned car, and when we think back on Medgar Evers, Emmett Till, and other victims of our own American violence here at home, we must ask ourselves: who is really backward?

Three hundred and thirty-four years ago, on a ship sailing to the New World, John Winthrop, who was to become the first Governor of Massachusetts, assembled the Puritans on the deck and said, "We must consider that we shall be as a city upon a hill, and the eyes of all people are upon us."

Never was that more true than today. The eyes of the world

are upon us, in Philadelphia, Mississippi, as well as Philadelphia, Pennsylvania; in Alabama and in New York; in the South and in the North.

The Puritans were in the middle of the Atlantic when John Winthrop talked to them of the new city that they would create in the new world. America is still in the middle of its journey. When millions of people suffer the injustice of discrimination and poverty, we know that we are only halfway to our goal, only halfway to the city upon the hill in which we all can take pride—a city and a country open to all men on merit alone, regardless of race, color, or creed.

2. Tokenism

This talk was given to the United Negro College Fund Symposium on the question of "Tokenism" in New York City on March 31, 1964.

WEBSTER DEFINES "tokenism" as "a partial payment made as a token of intention to pay the remainder of the debt later." To us here it has a newer meaning. Tokenism is today's "partial payment of a debt" *long overdue.* Whether it is opportunities for jobs, education, housing, or a better life generally, any group of American citizens given a "token" of such blessing is cheated. I am against "tokenism" because I am against cheating.

Yet, unfortunately, we are guilty of widespread cheating in America. Too many of our citizens have little more than a *token* opportunity to participate fully in many areas of our national life. A child's life expectancy at birth, how he is raised, his neighborhood, his home and his schools, how much a man can earn, how he earns it, and how he is permitted or required to spend it are matters frequently dictated by irrelevant criteria such as race.

But racial and religious groups are not our only minorities. There is an even larger minority—the poor, the poverty-stricken, the deprived of every race and color, of every religious belief, and in every section of our country. A booming economy has raised the living standards of a majority of our citizens. Our national income is at an all-time high. But we still have nine million families, black and white, with only a token participation in this good fortune, who are shut out from the economic benefits most Americans enjoy.

Indeed, the very technological advances responsible for the affluence of most have helped increase the miseries of the unskilled and the uneducated. Among these there are too many Negroes. Individual Negro income is less than 60 percent of the income of his white fellow citizen. The lifetime earnings expectation of a white man with less than eight years' schooling is $157,000. For the Negro it is $95,000. For the white man with twelve years of school it is $253,000; for the Negro, $151,000.

Many civil rights leaders in looking back on the New Deal realize that Franklin Roosevelt's programs for the solution of the nation's *economic* problems contributed more to the advancement of the Negro minority than any programs since the days of Abraham Lincoln. In attempting to solve the problems of the largest minority—the poor—Roosevelt contributed to the solution of the Negro's problems. Now, once again, we have turned our attention to the solution of the problems of our people in poverty. In so doing we will take an important step toward the complete emancipation of the Negro.

Last August, almost a quarter-million Americans gathered at the foot of the Lincoln Memorial in a dramatic demonstration of their determination to eliminate discrimination. From the list of demands on that occasion, I remember particularly Demand No. 7. It called for a "massive Federal program to train and place all unemployed workers, Negro *and* white, in meaningful and dignified jobs at decent wages." The fulfillment of this demand is the objective of President Johnson's War on Poverty.

The struggle for civil rights and the War Against Poverty

are thus all part of the same battle. It is a battle we have fought ever since a nation was established on the edge of a new continent. Other nations have had other reasons for existence. The American nation exists for this purpose: to open opportunity for its people. To the extent we have failed to bring opportunity to all, to that extent we have failed as a country and as a people. Tokenism—a grudging little effort here, a little help there—is not suited to the challenge, nor will it meet the need.

Recently, a Peace Corps Volunteer entered a small African village. A little boy pointed to him and said to his mother, "Look, there's a white man." "No, son," she said, "that's not a white man; that's a Peace Corps Volunteer."

We are working for the day when no one, anywhere, will say in this country, "Look, there is a white man," or "Look, there is a colored man," or "Look, there is a poor man."

We will see the day when they say only, "Look, there's an American."

3. A Tithe of Our Time

This appeal to the churches and great religions to provide specific new leadership was given to the National Conference on Religion and Race, held in Chicago, January 15, 1963.

IN A POWERFUL AND MOVING ESSAY James Baldwin has described an incident which happened to him only a few miles from here, at Chicago's O'Hare Airport. He and two Negro friends, all well over thirty, were refused service in the airport lounge on the pretense they were too young. After a long, noisy altercation, and after calling the manager, they were finally served. During the entire affair not one of the many white people in the lounge said a word to help. When it was all over, one of the Negroes, a Korean war veteran, turned to the young white man beside him and said, "You know, that fight was your fight, too." The young man replied, "I lost my conscience a long time ago," and turned and walked out.

The purpose of this meeting is to reawaken that conscience, to direct the power of religion to shaping the conduct and thoughts of men toward their brothers in a manner consistent with the compassion and love on which our spiritual tradition rests.

In so doing you follow in a great tradition. From the time of the ancient Hebrew prophets and the dispersal of the money-changers, men of God have taught us that social problems are moral problems on a huge scale, that a religion which did not struggle to remove oppression from the world of men would not be able to create the world of the spirit. This tradition is also deeply embedded in our own country's history. In the years preceding the proclamation of the emancipation whose centenary we celebrate now, men of God, of all faiths, North and South, took to pulpits, to press, and to public squares to demand an end to the moral evil of slavery.

Many religious leaders who followed this path were condemned by their congregations and deprived of their positions. Churches were burned and physical violence was often the reward of those who spoke freely. But their efforts were a significant force in ending slavery and in reshaping our society.

Today, a century later, we are given the same great opportunity. Today again the problem of racial wrongs and racial hatreds is the central moral problem of our republic. Today again hostility and misunderstanding, and even violence, await the man who attempts to translate the meaning of God's love into the actions and thoughts of men. Today again the hope for happiness of millions of Negro Americans can be profoundly affected by your efforts. And today again religion has one of those rare historical opportunities to renew its own purpose, enhance the dignity of its social role, and strengthen its institutions and its heritage by pitting itself against vast and powerful social forces which deny the role of God in the affairs of men.

As an official of the government, I am encouraged by a meeting like this. Justice for men is a common objective of religion and government and the exclusive domain of neither. I hope the traditional American regard for the separation of Church and State will never be interpreted as an excuse for either to pre-empt, or ignore, the vigorous pursuit of human dignity and freedom which are the legitimate concern of both Church *and* State.

But laws and government can deal only with the broadest and most obvious problems. They can guard against segregation in schools, but not against the thousands of incidents of discrimination and hatred which give the lie to what is learned in the schoolroom. They can carry sweeping mandates, but the process of their enforcement is so ponderous that it takes the entire energies of the nation to secure entrance of a single Negro into an unwilling white university.

Law can compel and even educate, yet in the last analysis the rule of law depends upon the convictions, desires, and judgments of the men it governs. Therefore we must look to those institutions whose task it is to teach moral values, to restate eternal principles in terms of today's conflicts, and to conform the daily conduct of men to the guiding values of justice, of love, and of compassion.

I find it alarming, therefore, when the government looks to the religious community for its share of the task and encounters, too often, a bland philosophy of *laissez faire*.

As a layman, for example, I wonder why I can go to church fifty-two times a year and not hear one sermon on the practical problems of race relations. I wonder why a conference like this does not lead to a continuing exchange of views and ideas and to a coordination of efforts to solve specific problems throughout the year. I wonder, furthermore, why each minister, rabbi, and priest does not map a specific program for his congregation, a program that will produce concrete gains over the next twelve months. Such a program could do many things.

It could bring to an end segregation in those churches and church schools where it exists. It could include a pledge to double the number of Negro families in the congregations where Negroes now attend. It could include the establishment of interracial councils where none exist. It could introduce

Negroes to every social and community event which the church sponsors or participates in. It could train lay Negro teachers and leaders to participate fully in congregational affairs.

If such a program, intended finally to bury religious *laissez faire* in racial problems, were instituted, it would encourage each member of the congregation to pledge a *tithe of his time* to removing racial barriers at work, at play, and at worship.

I wonder why an appeal requesting every church member to give a tithe of time has not been made already. It is easier to give a tithe of your money than a tithe of your time. Isn't the time you give of yourself more important than the money? Do our churches expect too little of their members in solving race problems?

Suppose five thousand congregations in America were to set up volunteer groups to combat racial prejudice and eliminate racial tensions in five thousand religious precincts throughout America. And suppose the five thousand were to become ten thousand or twenty thousand?

In thousands of communities religiously inspired volunteers would be inviting Negro families to personal social functions. They would be organizing and joining interracial councils, securing entrance of Negroes into previously all-white neighborhoods, ensuring enforcement of constitutional rights to equal opportunity, and improving living conditions in segregated neighborhoods.

A profound new force would be at work in America, emanating from the deepest wells of religious inspiration and reaching for the noblest summits of human aspiration. That combination would be invincible.

Some critics will want to ignore the church's word on the thesis that it is irrelevant, like the corporation president who said, "Of course, segregation is wrong from the Christian point of view. Let's not discuss it from *that* point of view."

Efforts by churches and synagogues have illustrated what can be accomplished. After his school system was integrated, one Kentucky superintendent said, "I believe ministers and lay church leaders made the greatest contribution in getting the general public to accept desegregation."

You may be familiar with the experience in St. Louis. The six-hundred-member Church Federation set aside a Sunday for thanksgiving prayer for public school desegregation. It challenged pastors and membership to take an open stand for integration. The Cardinal called in a general letter for all Catholic pastors to influence their hundreds of thousands of parishioners to cooperate. The Rabbinical Association urged all citizens to work and pray for its success.

On the other hand, we know what can happen when religious leadership is absent. Remember Clinton, Tennessee? Violence erupted there when desegregation was attempted. It took 650 National Guardsmen to restore order after days of tension. When a special report was written to analyze what had happened it was found that "Churches were not utilized to any extent in Clinton, Tennessee."

During the crisis a Baptist minister escorted Negro students through the howling crowds. He was beaten by the mob, but his courage was unshaken. What might have happened in Clinton had the religious community rallied to support him? One man is not enough.

There is no reliable justice without the machinery of justice —the government. But the machinery of justice cannot be effective without men and women who have the will and character to make it work.

The maxim is true that politics is the art of the possible. The constant challenge we face in politics is to enlarge the area of the possible. To do that requires that men change their objectives. But they can't change their objectives unless they change their prejudices, and that requires changes in men's minds, and that requires changes in men's hearts, and the human heart is the business of religion.

We can achieve equality if religion permeates its adherents

with an urgent sense of personal responsibility for ending the injustice of our present system.

If I have any justification to speak to this august body, it is to encourage you to make a conscious, deliberate assault on racial and religious barriers. From our experience in the Peace Corps, I know those barriers are vulnerable.

We sent a Chinese-American doctor to Ghana. When he rose to speak to his students, they couldn't believe he was from the United States—"that place across the sea where no colored man can go to school." They thought he was a Chinese Communist.

In Nepal we sent four Volunteers to teach in a small college. Three of them were visited one night by a young Marxist student who had studied in Peking and who had already won a scholarship to Lumumba University in Moscow. This student had also just been elected to a place on the important "panchayat" council which runs the city government.

He came to rib the Volunteers about discrimination in America. Just then Carl Jorgenson walked in—a tall, young Negro, a top graduate of Harvard, the son of a leader of the NAACP in Washington. "Sure, let's talk about it," he said. And they did. The young Marxist, stunned that Americans would let a Negro into the Peace Corps, that a Negro could graduate from Harvard, that he could be living with three white Americans, has come back time and time again to discuss America with the Volunteers.

There is only one real explanation of our success in the field of race relations. We made a deliberate effort to change old patterns.

Let me close with a pledge and a request.

We in government will continue our efforts. We will move with all the instruments at our command to achieve justice among men. That is our pledge.

My request is: Help us. If there is to be a social order allowing the fullest possible development of individual personality, if there is to be the widest and deepest possible fellowship among men of different races, we need what Maritain has called Democracy of the Person. You can bring it about. Help us to see our task. Stir our consciences. Inspire and challenge us to take our principles into the toughest walks of life and make them work.

4. The Roots of Racism

On August 29, 1958, Sargent Shriver inaugurated the First National Catholic Conference for Interracial Justice. As Conference Chairman, he participated in the drafting of the resolutions, which called for action against de facto housing segregation in the North and for effective school integration. This was his keynote address.

MOST OF MY LIFE I have had a great hero, St. Paul, the author of so many hard sayings. You remember his words: "There is neither Gentile nor Jew, circumcised nor uncircumcised, Barbarian nor Scythian, bond nor free. But Christ is all and in all."

To follow Christ's leadership, to imitate Him, speak the truth as He did, is the toughest job in the world. But that, it seems to me, is precisely our job. It is our job to speak the truth as plainly as we can. It is our job to reaffirm, to the best of our ability, the fundamental Christian principles concerning justice between men of different races or nationalities. We must try to apply those principles to specific, concrete problems of contemporary American life. The commissions of this convention on housing, schools, employment, and on parochial life must speak out loud and clear.

But let us suppose that one year or ten years, or even twenty years, from now educational opportunity in all American schools were truly equalized and raised to the highest standards of intellectual achievement. Let us suppose that discrimination in employment were gone, that ghettos were gone, that all Americans enjoyed equal and excellent opportunities for health and hospital care, for employment, for housing. Would we then have eliminated racial prejudice? The answer, I fear, is No.

The sad truth is that racial prejudice and injustice would still be with us. Even if we achieved every one of our current goals, even if we erased all the existing external indications of racial prejudice and discrimination, we would still have the disease inside, festering like a cancer, needing constant treatment and remedial care.

Racism cannot be cured solely by attacking some of the results it produces, like discrimination in housing or in education. True, we need effective programs to reduce such discrimination. Action in these areas is necessary, appropriate, and justified. But we must also treat the disease of racism itself. And this means we must understand the disease. For racism is an immensely complicated phenomenon. It is an affliction of the spirit, of the soul of man, rather than a disease of his conscious, intellectual life. That is one reason why racists are so irrational and illogical in their attempts to justify their prejudices.

The roots of racism lie deep in man's nature. The secret sources of racism, to quote that eminent teacher and philosopher, Yves Simon, lie deep in man's greed for a cheap labor supply—deep in man's insecurity about his own means of livelihood—deep in man's desire for aristocratic distinction, his desire to feel that he is a member of a distinguished people, an elite better than other human beings—deep in his anxiety to be somebody, to belong to a group which does not include everyone, to be free of his fear of sinking into the great, struggling, undifferentiated mass of humanity. Even warped religious feelings can produce racism. Jews, for example, have suffered persecution from misguided Christians.

History is full of pitiful examples of misguided efforts to create selected groups among the peoples of the world: the phony racial elite set up by Adolf Hitler; the discredited doctrine of Karl Marx establishing an elite of the working class; the Brahman elite of the Hindu caste system; the bourgeois elite of wealth; or even the Grecian elite composed of intellectual men.

All these efforts to separate men failed. All similar efforts will fail because they are based on materialistic desires for money, or security, or power, or success in this world. None of them recognizes that the only true superiority, the only genuine elite, in this world, or in the next, is the elite of those men and women who have given their lives to justice and to charity.

We must never forget or minimize the spiritual side of our nature and of our mission for interracial justice and charity. The Communists and the Fascists abroad all degrade man. They make him a mere pawn in the struggle for power. They treat him not as a person, but as an object. You use an object; you love a person.

St. Paul saw that without charity we ourselves become objects, sounding brass and tinkling cymbals. It is love that crowns man with his true dignity, and the giving of love even more than the receiving. It is as persons that we communicate with each other. It is as objects that we clash with each other. Without the love that St. Paul envisaged, the world is a clashing of object against object, class against class, tyrant against tyrant, race against race. With St. Paul's type of love, we are persons—deep calling to deep, the human heart speaking to human heart. With this love we have in ourselves the width of the universe. In this love is the only complete freedom that man can ever have.

To determine whether we are actually succeeding in this, we can evaluate our efforts with a practical test, a test that may be applied to any organization devoted to interracial justice: Does it establish communication between man and man, each in his full independence and integrity and difference? I have said "communication." I could use a more ancient word, full of implications, the word "communion."

Those who hold the kind of communion between man and man that marks the full acceptance of each man in his uniqueness as a person cannot be content with either the exaggeration of differences or the simplification of them. Rather, the ideal of a Catholic Interracial Council wants the many to be one, in those things that matter most deeply, and yet to remain many. It wants the full sound of the orchestra, the harmony of the many different notes; it wants the full range of the spectrum, no one color being of any special beauty in itself, but all being beautiful together.

This is to define the mission in its full difficulty, because it defines the mission in its full humanity. I would say that this is a dangerously high ideal to put before ourselves, in the day-to-day work of this organization, except that anything less than this is even more dangerous. For anything less than this takes man as something less than man, as something to be manipulated by the tyrant.

A Catholic Interracial Council is not a council of one side against another; it is not a council for the advancement or protection of this people or that; but—to borrow the motto of one of our great foundations—it is a council for the advancement of man, for the advancement of man in his understanding of what it is to be a man, in himself and in others.

Charles Péguy, the great French author, in discussing the persecutions inflicted upon the Jewish people throughout the ages, penned these memorable words:

"I know this people, the Jewish people, well. On its skin it has no single spot which is not painful, where is not some old bruise, some old contusion, some silent woe, the memory of a silent woe, a scar, a wound, a laceration from Orient to Occident. . . ."

Let us dedicate ourselves to the binding up of those old

wounds, whether they be on the backs of white men, Negroes, yellow men, or Jews. Let us erase the memory of those silent woes, those scars, those lacerations. Let us create a true community.

5. To Be True Knights of Columbus

On February 24, 1964, civil rights workers planned to picket the large annual Knights of Columbus Dinner in Chicago because no Negroes were members. Picketing was called off when it was learned that Sargent Shriver was coming to urge the inclusion of Negroes, Puerto Ricans, and other colored Americans in the K. of C.

YOU OF THE KNIGHTS OF COLUMBUS have tremendous potential for good in Chicago, but not only in Chicago. The big news these days is Cuba, Castro, Communism in Latin America. What are the Knights of Columbus doing about Latin Americans? About the one-third of all the Catholics in the world who live there?

What language did Christopher Columbus speak? Spanish— the language of most South Americans and of millions of Americans on United States soil.

What are the Knights of Columbus doing to communicate with the Spanish-speaking people in Chicago? How many Puerto Rican, Spanish-speaking Americans are in this audience tonight? How many are members of the Knights of Columbus?

What about the Latin Americans who are full-blooded Indians? Guatemala, for example, is populated by people 80 percent of whom are full-blooded Indians. Would they meet any North American Indians in the Knights of Columbus?

And what about the millions of Catholic Negroes in Latin America? Journalists and politicians swarm and hover over Cuba, vying with one another for credit or charging one another with blame. But what are we doing about Brazil, one hundred times bigger and more important than Cuba? Are we helping Brazil? Would a Brazilian Catholic Negro be welcome here tonight? And what about a Negro American from Chicago?

The greatest burden carried by both Eisenhower and Kennedy in their dealings with Latin Americans is our failure as North Americans to respect the Spanish culture, the Indian heritage, the multiracial background of most Latin peoples. These peoples, frankly, honestly, but politely, don't believe we want them as friends and equals. In their eyes, North Americans, even their co-religionists, show very few signs of treating South Americans, American Indians, or Negroes as equals.

It is in this kind of psychological and spiritual atmosphere that Communism grows and spreads like cancer. Are we actually nurturing Communism in Latin America by our actions and attitudes in North America?

These are hard questions, perhaps impolite, rude questions tonight. But these are the questions I have to answer all over South and Central America, all over Africa, all over Asia.

So far I have always answered that we North Americans do believe in the equality of all men; we do believe that "all men are created equal"; we do believe, and are willing to practice, the principles of our Declaration of Independence, our Constitution.

In Indonesia Foreign Minister Subandrio said to me, "Do the people of the United States, do the Peace Corps Volunteers, really believe in the equality of all peoples? Are you sincerely ready to respect diverse, different races of men, different cultures, different languages, different methods of organizing society?" I said yes.

To be sure, these men and others like them all over Latin America, and Africa, and Asia, want our help financially. They want, and desperately need, dollars and factories and power plants. But they can take our money and hate us—hate our culture, hate our superior attitude, hate our hypocrisy, hate our power. And they will hate us if, by our actions at home and abroad, we convince them that we do not respect them as racial equals, cultural equals, political equals, as human beings fully equal to us.

In Latin America the Communist propaganda machine tells the world every day that we are not what we say we are. They point to racial segregation. They point to the huge American industrial companies in Latin America and claim we are only interested in making money out of Venezuelan oil, or Chilean copper, or Bolivian tin. They point to our military campaigns against Mexico, against Nicaragua, against Panama, against Haiti, against Puerto Rico. This is the food on which Castro feeds.

Let us remember that this current struggle may well be solved without armed conflict or exchange or nuclear blows. Khrushchev is committed to this very proposition. He believes the Soviet Union can win without a shooting war. Never forget that Cuba became a Communist state without the help of a single Russian or Chinese soldier.

Time has now run out. We no longer can enjoy the luxury of debate on what happened in China or Cuba. We must act, as a nation and as individuals, to guarantee that the future will not be a repetition of the past.

Catholics have been asked to join the Papal Volunteers for service especially in Latin America. Protestants are being encouraged by their various denominations to go abroad as lay missionaries. Businessmen are being asked by the federal government to invest more of their capital in private enterprise in Latin America. And Peace Corps Volunteers are at work in eighteen countries south of the border. But these are only a part of the effort we must make. We must now uncover in this country and in Latin America the vitality, energy, and strength necessary to shape this hemisphere's destiny.

Scarcely a month before Castro imposed a dictatorship on the Cuban people, Pope John told the National Catholic Congress in Cuba: "The face of the earth could change if true charity reigned: the charity of the Christian who shares the sorrow, the suffering of the unfortunate, who seeks their happiness, their salvation, as well as his own. The charity of the Christian, convinced that what he owns has a social function, and that to use what is superfluous to his need in favor of one who does not have the necessities, is not an optional generosity, but a duty."

I have seen the Maryknoll priests from Philadelphia, Boston, and Chicago working with the Indians high in the mountains of the Andes. I have seen them organizing credit unions and savings and loan associations in the slums of Santiago, Arequipa, and Lima. The Franciscans are there, the Sisters of Mercy from Chicago are there, and the Sacret Heart nuns, too. But the magnitude of the challenge far surpasses the size of their response, or ours.

Almost 200 million people live to the south of us. The population is expanding faster than in any other region in the world. The average income of these people is one-ninth that of a citizen of the United States. But statistics are cold. They cannot describe the daily fight for life, the endless struggles to break those ancient bonds of hunger, disease, ignorance, and poverty.

Fifteen months ago I visited a slum outside of Lima, Peru, called "The Mountain." More than twenty thousand people lived on this mountain. When I got there, I found out that The Mountain was a mountain of garbage. Yet the people living there were not corrupt or depraved. The men were not loafers, or the women sluts. By and large they were decent, respectable people feverishly seeking work, willing to do anything to improve their lot.

Outside of Rio de Janeiro in Brazil and Caracas, Venezuela, I have stood in the slums on the mountainsides at night and looked down upon sights as fabulous as anything in the *Arabian Nights*—glamorous neon signs, four-lane highways, soaring sky-scrapers, beautiful homes, cabarets, fine restaurants. But where I stood, in the slums, lived three-fourths of all the people, and three-fourths of all the people had neither electricity, nor clean water, nor sewers, nor telephones, nor schools, nor hospitals, nor food, nor hope for the future.

After one such evening I said to myself, "If I were a Communist agitator and could not start a revolution in one of those slums in eight months, I'd quit my job."

The big electric signs at night, the tall skyscrapers, the fancy automobiles, all have English words written on them: *Firestone, Sears Roebuck, Esso, Frigidaire, Coca-Cola.* The signs of wealth are always in English, while the signs of poverty are written in Spanish or Portuguese.

It's so easy to explain that contrast in terms of exploitation by the Gringos from the North. It's so easy when those Gringos isolate themselves. It's so easy when thousands of those Gringos profited financially for years, and still can't speak the local language, or eat the local food. It's so easy when Radio Havana nightly explains the difference between the "haves" and the "have-nots" in the gross simplicities but forceful sentences of Marxism and Communism.

Today a pitifully small band of priests and Catholic organizations are struggling against these elements, struggling to bring about a better life for the people. But let's face the facts. The Church has not always been on the side of the people. Far too often it has been identified with the status quo, the rich and the powerful, and those who opposed social reforms and political democracy.

The situation is changing, but is the change coming too late?

In every country of Latin America there are Catholic priests and laymen fighting lonely battles to educate the ignorant, feed the hungry, and house the poor. They are in the forefront of the struggle. But these are not just Catholics; they are free men helping other men to gain freedom—freedom from human tyranny as well as freedom from poverty, disease, and illiteracy. One proof is the overwhelmingly hospitable welcome they have accorded to the Peace Corps Volunteers—Protestant, Jew, agnostic, atheist, as well as Catholic—who have come to Latin America.

In Chile, in Peru, and in Honduras, priests have frequently provided lodgings and food until the Peace Corps Volunteers could get a place to live. And in one place, a Jewish Peace Corps Volunteer has refused to move from the home of the priest where he had been living from the beginning, because, as he said, everyone in the village had begun to call him "Padre" and he is getting a 25 percent discount at all the stores.

But to assist in this struggle you don't have to serve in the Peace Corps. We, the citizens of the richest nation in the history of the world, are all responsible—directly and personally responsible—for helping the millions in Latin America.

This is not a responsibility which can be left in the hands of the government while we pursue our daily lives and comforts. It is not a responsibility which can be avoided by criticizing foreign aid or applauding the Peace Corps.

Rather as individuals and organizations, we must personally give of our own resources and, what is even more difficult, of our own time. Therefore, I propose that every diocesan chapter of the Knights of Columbus adopt a diocese in Latin America, that you make the work of that diocese an object of your own personal concern and charity. In this way you can give material assistance to the efforts of individual priests and laymen. You can provide Latin Americans an opportunity for education, either in their own country or here in the United States. Your experience and knowledge can be of direct help to those in your adopted diocese who are trying to organize a union, start a business, or launch an agricultural cooperative.

You and your children will thus have an opportunity to broaden your horizons through learning, in a direct and intimate way, of the problems and life of people in other lands. For we have much to learn in the way of the mind and spirit from our brothers in Latin America who have kept alive their deep beliefs despite an adversity which is almost beyond our capacity to imagine. Thus this effort, by bringing us closer to other men, will bring us closer to God.

VI

HEALTH

AND

EDUCATION

"It is man who is important, not the machine
. . . it is man who is the object of all our efforts."
— PABLO CASALS

On June 6, 1964, a brass band saw me off on a flight from Hart-ford to Boston. This was an unusual brass band. The musicians were from the Mansfield Training School in Mansfield, Con-necticut. They were all mentally retarded. Listening to their music, looking at them, you would never suspect any of them was retarded.

Fifty years ago no one would have bothered to teach them to play musical instruments—or anything else. They would have been treated like wild animals, some even kept in chains. They would certainly not have been there in the Hartford air terminal serenading someone because he happened to have worked with the Joseph P. Kennedy, Jr., Memorial Foundation. My wife should have been there because she has been the true inspira-tion for this effort.

For ten years she and I have been working with leaders on this medical frontier and other aspects of medicine, at all levels, from research to practice, from institutes and medical schools to hospitals and sanitariums. Now in the Peace Corps there are some eighty-four doctors serving on the staff in forty-five coun-tries, and there are medical projects requiring a growing number of Volunteer doctors, nurses, and hospital or public health tech-nicians. Medicine is an essential element in any humane twen-tieth-century society.

Another vital element is education, which was the subject

157

of most of the talking or writing I did while President of the Board of Education of Chicago in the years before 1960. The editor has cut most of the statistics about appropriations secured, bonds voted, schools built, and teachers employed. But in these fields the great test—how we treat the least of us, how we treat the individual human being most in need—will only be passed if the practical tests of taxes, budgets, and payrolls are passed first.

1. Roads Back to a More Human Medicine

On the 100th Anniversary of the Boston City Hospital, on June 4, 1964, this appeal was made to the "general practitioner" and to the medical profession generally.

LAST WINTER in Honduras a Peace Corps doctor was walking through the streets of a mountain village. As I watched him, the scene developed like a story in the Bible. People came flocking out of their houses bringing the lame, the halt, and the blind. A woman said, "Doctor, look at my baby!" An old man exhibited his leg. The doctor stopped occasionally to pat a child, comfort a mother. He knew practically everybody, and they knew him—and loved him.

Later, I mentioned this incident to my wife. She said, "Why, that's the way everything was right here in the United States—before civilization!"

That is the way things were "before civilization," before specialization, when the business of doctors was the entire person, not *parts* of a person.

I have several proposals to take us back to the humanity we had in medicine "before civilization."

This hospital's hundred-year life span divides almost equally: fifty years before the revolution in American medicine caused by the famous Flexner Report on medical education, and fifty years following that report.

During the first fifty years of this hospital's life, much of American medicine was in poor shape. Medical schools were inadequate. Educational standards were almost nonexistent. Quack practitioners were everywhere. Scientific research was not being related to medicine.

Then in 1910 came the famous Flexner Report. As a result, 150 medical schools in America were pared down to 50. A college education became a prerequisite for medical school entrance. Science came in, in a big way.

As a result of this revolution, we have made incredible advances in medical science: we have raised life expectancies, slashed maternity mortality rates, and ended the threat of many diseases.

But it seems that at the same time we have lost something of the human dimension in medicine. Doctors have had to specialize more and more. Their training has become more complicated and time-consuming.

It is like the ever-expanding universe. The doctors are spinning off into science, research, and specialization faster than the patients can keep up with them. Doctors are staying in the big cities where all the best facilities are located for both training and practice. The more specialized they become, the more they tend to gravitate away from rural communities that need them to cities overcrowded with specialists. And there they may become so absorbed in their specialty that they really lose contact with the throngs of patients.

So part of our problem today seems to be to get these doctors "talking to people" again. One of my proposals tonight, in an attempt to reverse this trend, is: Join the Peace Corps. Return to the grass-roots kind of medical practice that is possible in the Peace Corps. We need doctors in the Peace Corps more than specialists. And the specialists who have come into the Peace

Corps tell us they have rediscovered their capacity to be doctors.

We need just plain country doctors—in the literal sense, because a doctor in the Peace Corps often has to cover a whole country. He needs a "roadside manner" as much as a "bedside manner."

John King, a twenty-six-year-old Peace Corps staff doctor, graduated from Yale to paying "house calls" on Peace Corps Volunteers in Tanganyika, five hundred miles apart.

Franz Koning, one of our Volunteer doctors in Sierra Leone, came to the Peace Corps from Seattle, Washington, where he was a general practitioner. In a single day in the Magburaka Hospital Clinic in Sierra Leone he examined 150 men, women, and children. These are some of the things he diagnosed: twenty-five cases of malaria, one case of TB, three tropical ulcers, one yaws, eight cases of combined malaria and roundworm, one gonorrhea, one skinworm, one schistosomiasis, three snake bites. There were also five cases of multiple tropical disease, including anemia, beriberi, pellagra, malaria, malnutrition, roundworms; one case of gonorrheal conjunctivitis, four abscesses, one fracture, one burn. Now that was on a Monday. Tuesday through Saturday it was just routine business, like elephantiasis, leprosy, polio, meningitis.

Just a few weeks ago, Dr. Bob Cooke, the head of pediatrics at Johns Hopkins, said in a speech dedicating a new children's medical center that diseases like rickets and scurvy were rarities in America in 1964. "Today," Dr. Cooke said, "the presentation of a case of vitamin D deficiency rickets or scurvy would be a 'cause célèbre,' attended by a full quota of house staff and students!"

Well, we put on this kind of presentation in the Peace Corps every day of the week, and we would be delighted to have "a full quota of house staff and students" attend and stay awhile.

Franz Koning, along with five Peace Corps nurses, and Dave

Griffith, another Volunteer doctor from the Yale Medical School, have given a great boost to the Magburaka Hospital. Patients are coming there from all over Sierra Leone, walking, flying, or riding buses. One mother and father came there on foot from twenty miles away carrying an infant who was suffering from an abdominal hernia. The Peace Corps medical team is handling all this without much fancy medical equipment. When one of our Washington staff members visited them and asked if they needed anything, they said yes. They needed not an electroencephalogram, not a heart-lung machine, not a vacuum extractor. They said, "Get us rags. We need rags to help keep things clean around here. There are no rags in this country."

Then you go up the West African coast a little and you come to Togo, a country that had only ten doctors. In Sokode, an up-country town, we have twenty Volunteers, including doctors, nurses, lab technicians, and a pharmacist. This medical team is operating the Sokode Hospital almost alone. In addition, they are carrying out public health programs in the area, running clinics in surrounding villages, teaching hygiene in the schools. This whole project was put together by Nick Cunningham, a pediatrician in his mid-thirties who came to us from the Indian Health Division of the Public Health Service. Nick personally set up the program, then recruited a surgeon, a generalist, another pediatrician, a pharmacist, and fifteen nurses—from all over the country.

What Nick Cunningham and other doctors have been finding out in the Peace Corps is something too often forgotten in the medical profession in America. First of all they have been dealing with the individual as a whole, not just as a gall bladder or as a right ventricle. They have been working as general practitioner, surgeon, diagnostician, and psychiatrist all at the same time. They have been getting away from the technology of medicine and back to the art of medicine—the art of dealing with people.

And they have been learning the challenge and fascination

of preventive medicine that deals directly with human beings. In this country preventive medicine has become so sophisticated that it deals generally with "things"—with pollution of streams or of the air, with community resources, with radiation control. Curative medicine is the chief attraction for medical students in America because the teaching of preventive medicine has become dry and uninteresting.

But there is nothing dry or uninteresting about seeing 150 patients, all with dramatic symptoms, during a long day in an African clinic. Exhausting, yes, but never dull.

Many of our Peace Corps doctors are coming back with a renewed interest in "human" medicine—in general practice, in dealing with people in the old "family doctor" way. Many who never dreamed of it before now want to go into public health, into preventive medicine.

These doctors are going to have an impact on medical practice in America, perhaps as much impact on our own communities back home as they had overseas. If they practice the same kind of medicine in Council Bluffs, Iowa, as they did in Dar es Salaam, Tanganyika, America will have gained as much as these doctors have given abroad.

But this impact could be much greater if the medical profession were to join the Peace Corps in a partnership—a partnership that would provide a two-year "residency" in a "school of general practice" conducted by Peace Corps doctors in forty-six countries around the globe. Their training would be not only in surgery, not only in obstetrics and pediatrics, but in compassion, in patience, in endurance, in resourcefulness. And there would be times when their only equipment would be their hands; their only anesthetic, a soothing voice; their only specialty, empathy.

All of this is broadening and humanizing for a doctor, but he does not have to go to Sarawak, or Nepal, or Nyasaland to get this kind of experience. The same kind of opportunity, the same kind of challenge, the same kind of need still exist in some areas of this country. And that is my second proposal for a road back to a more "human" medicine.

We need doctors in the program to wipe out poverty in the United States. This involves going out to the people—to thirty million people in this country. It involves taking medicine to some places almost deserted or at least rarely visited by doctors.

Poverty is not just a problem of nonwhites; nearly 80 percent of the poor are white. And it's not strictly a problem of city slums; about 50 percent of the poor live on farms and in rural areas. In the rural areas of Alabama, Mississippi, Arkansas, South Carolina, and Georgia, 25 to 40 percent of the mothers give birth to their babies unattended by physicians.

President Johnson's program against poverty will offer doctors and nurses a real chance for service to humanity, at its neediest, in our desperately poor rural areas, among our migratory workers, or on Indian reservations—on all those frontiers still largely untouched by progress.

Eventually the government may be able to offer service in the War Against Poverty, as well as service for Volunteer doctors in the Peace Corps, as an alternative to regular military service. Meanwhile, the medical profession could give great impetus to our efforts in two ways: Volunteer doctors in the Peace Corps could be given additional credit with their specialty boards for work done overseas. And young doctors could be permitted to take an official one-year residency in some area of the antipoverty program in the United States. This would combine their academic training with a firsthand experience unavailable elsewhere.

My third proposal tonight has nothing to do directly with the Peace Corps or the poverty program. It has to do with American society, with the character of American life. The medical profession in this country has been getting more and more insulated from the rest of American life. Everything in it focuses on professionalism. Too many doctors talk only to other doctors; they go only to doctors' meetings, doctors' parties, doctors' conventions. People outside the profession are seen only as patients. In this country we seldom see doctors in other fields.

A study of the recent Eighty-fifth Congress showed that in the House of Representatives there were 234 lawyers, 49 businessmen, 23 educators, 23 journalists, 23 former state or local officials, 20 farmers, 16 real estate and insurance people, 7 former Congressional aides—and only 5 doctors, and 1 dentist. The doctors were tied with the bankers and the advertising and public relations people, but at least they beat out the funeral directors!

In other countries it is a different story.

In Indonesia Foreign Minister Subandrio is a doctor, so is the Minister for Private Banks and Capital, and so are six other top officials. In South Vietnam the Minister for Foreign Affairs, the Vice Prime Minister, the Minister of State, and others are doctors. The President of Argentina, ex-president Kubitschek, and the Secretary of Agriculture of Brazil, the Chilean Minister of the Interior, two Vice Presidents of Costa Rica are all doctors. This is true in many other countries where education is generalized and not so heavily concentrated on the highly scientific aspects of medicine.

In Peru the growing number of the "sons of Hippocrates" in public life, and the decrease in lawyers and other "traditional" politicians, caused the Arequipa newspaper *El Pueblo* to comment: "The hour of the doctors has arrived. Suddenly the quiet man of the white apron . . . has left the clinics and the hospitals and has come to the battleground of civic action."

Here in this country, doctors in public life would have a different exposure to humanity. They would get new insights into the needs of all our people. Likewise, doctors would be in a better position to advise our policymakers and appreciate their problems as we try to make a better society.

In the Peace Corps we have some doctors serving overseas not as doctors but as full-time administrators. Dr. Charles Houston, for example. Dr. Houston was a *magna cum laude* graduate of Harvard, then *magna cum laude* again at the Columbia School of Physicians and Surgeons in 1935. During World War II, he was a Navy flight surgeon. Just before he came into the Peace Corps in 1962, Dr. Houston was working as a cardiologist at the Aspen Clinic in Colorado. One of his hobbies, mountain climbing and exploring, had taken him to India and Pakistan a few years ago. That got him interested in the plight of impoverished people overseas—and in the Peace Corps. So in 1962 he took his wife Dorcas, a nurse, and his three children to India, where he has been running a complex Peace Corps program of 250 Volunteers.

Here was a man who had over a quarter of a century of varied medical practice, and still he knew there was another kind of experience he wanted, another world outside the world of clinics, waiting rooms, and operating theaters. No one ought to train and work, live and die, under one professional roof. Everyone ought to see how the "other half" lives. A lot of the staff members who came to the Peace Corps were lawyers, newspapermen, educators, legislators. They were men seeking a meaningful interlude in the normal routine of their lives, a new exposure. And above all they were men who wanted to work with people, not away from them, nor with things.

In a nation that devotes 5 percent of its Gross National Product to health and medicine, how can medical people neglect to take a bigger part in public life, whether on a local, state, or national level?

These are the three broad avenues back to a more human kind of medicine, avenues that lead away from the special and back to the general: the Peace Corps, the poverty program, and public life. As Albert Einstein said, "It is not enough that you should understand about applied science in order that your work may increase man's blessings. Concern for man himself, and his fate, must always form the chief interest of all technical endeavors."

2. The Favorite Pupil

This fragment of a talk given on March 21, 1957, to the Chicago Council on the Mentally Handicapped conveys the human agony of families, like the Kennedy family, faced with a child suffering mental retardation. The Kennedy Foundation, which in the last fifteen years has contributed thirteen million dollars in this field, has been the chief financial and organizing instrument of the effort to prevent or to cure retardation, and to bring the mentally retarded into useful places in society.

THE COMMANDER IN CHIEF of our Mediterranean Fleet, Admiral Charles Brown, tells a remarkable story about a nine-year-old boy, the son of John Puerifoy, formerly our Ambassador to Greece. The child's name was Clinton, and he was a spastic.

"He was a brilliant lad," recalls Admiral Brown, "and deeply appealing." Queen Frederika grew fond of the boy while the Puerifoys were stationed in Greece, and often asked him for long visits to the Royal Palace in Athens.

During these visits young Clinton Puerifoy played freely with Queen Frederika's two children. One day, Prince Constantine said to his little American friend, "My sister and I have been talking about you, and we have decided that you must be the favorite pupil of Jesus."

"What do you mean?" asked Clinton.

"Well," replied the Prince, "you know how it is. In school the best pupil is always given the hardest problems to solve. God gave you the hardest problem of all, so you must be his favorite pupil."

With sudden tears in his eyes, the crippled child replied, "I don't believe you!"

That night the Queen sat on the edge of Clint's bed as she tucked him in. She said, "I heard what the Prince told you today, and I agree with him. I believe you are a favorite pupil of Jesus."

For a moment, two troubled eyes stared back at her. Then Clint said, "I don't believe it! I won't believe it unless my Daddy says that he believes it!"

Later, Queen Frederika told Jack Puerifoy the story. The Ambassador shook his head and said, "I can't tell him I believe that. I cannot believe that a good and just God would do that to my little boy."

Two thousand years ago another story was written: "And Jesus passing by," the story begins in St. John's Gospel, "saw a man blind from his birth. And His disciples asked Him: 'Rabbi, who hath sinned, this man or his parents, that he should be born blind?' Jesus answered: 'Neither hath this man sinned, nor his parents; but that the works of God should be made manifest in him.' "

We have no record of the immediate reaction to these words. But down the ages many have replied as Dostoevsky's Ivan Karamazov did, "If God's truth demands the tortured cry of even one innocent child, then God's truth is not worth the price of admission."

Others have said that guiltless suffering for adults or children should be ended. "Mercy killing" is the mellifluous phrase used by some; "improvement of the race" is the argument of those who believe in enforced eugenics; efficiency, economy, productivity were the rallying cries of Hitler or Stalin, whose economic and cultural theories eliminated any place for the blind, crippled, aged, or mentally retarded.

But here in America, thank God, the overwhelming majority has not been seduced by these arguments. Instead, we have adopted in substance and in fact the standards, the thinking, and the ideals of the Rabbi of the Gospel.

"The Christian inspiration in dealing with 'exceptional children,' " an eminent American clergyman reminds us, "is very different from that of any other civilization. It might be summed up in the proposition that the measure of the degree of a community's civilization, as Christians understand civilization, is what we may call the 'test of the least.' "

What provision does a civilization make for its least members? What advantage does it offer for those who are least able to take care of themselves? Jesus said, "For as long as you did it to one of these my least brethren, you did it to me."

Pagans believed that their gods were pleased by the progress of the best, by those who could be exceptionally independent. When Jesus spoke about the least, a new concept dawned as to what constitutes a civilized community. With us the test of the worth of a community is not how well the most privileged people make out, but what provision is made for the least, for those who are exceptional in their need for our kindness.

You teachers of the mentally retarded are meeting this test. You have dedicated your lives to the service of the least in mental capacity, the least in physical endowment, the least in years, the least in all things people covet for their children.

In this work, it should be noted, you are serving the cause of education. You are teachers—teachers in the same manner and tradition as the two greatest teachers of all time, Christ and Socrates. Neither of them taught in a university. Neither of them concentrated on research. Neither of them confined his conversation and action to philosophers or to doctors of education or to men of power.

Socrates taught in the market place of Athens. He taught the ignorant, the unpowerful, often the "least," if you will, of Athenian citizens. It is typical that he begins his famous questions with the words, "Tell me, Stranger . . ."

Christ wasted little time with the doctors of the law or with the Pharisees. He taught the deaf, dumb, blind, and lame; He spoke mostly to the multitudes, not to the elite.

When you devote your time to the mentally retarded, you are selecting the most difficult students to inspire. You are working where the work is hardest, and the compensations sometimes least. But in doing this work you can be sure of the gratitude and thanks of parents, children, and the public. You are giving your lives to make sure that even the least of our children shall enjoy to the maximum of their capacity the full fruits of educated living. More than this no teacher can do.

3. Mental Retardation: A Twentieth-Century Challenge

This is the keynote address to the first White House Confer-
ence on Mental Retardation, held on September 19, 1963, and
attended by leaders of medicine and mental retardation pro-
grams from over forty states.

In 1922, Sinclair Lewis published *Babbitt;* Rudolph Valentino played in *Blood and Sand;* and "Toot, Toot, Tootsie!" was at the top of the hit parade. There were probably few who knew, or even had heard of, Niels Bohr or knew of the discovery for which he had just been honored. Sixteen years later, in 1938, the name of Enrico Fermi rang few bells in the minds of Americans, most of whom were taking their children to see a new film called *Snow White and the Seven Dwarfs.* Fermi's Nobel Prize for his work in nuclear fission went virtually unnoticed by people who were applauding the return of Neville Chamberlain, home from Munich with "Peace in Our Time."

Throughout the roaring twenties and the depression-ridden thirties, few Americans, consumed with problems at home and dim threats abroad, were aware that in laboratories all over the world scientists were laying the foundation for a revolution in the physical sciences—a revolution which has shaped and is shaping our lives far more importantly than all the activities of the statesmen and dictators, songwriters and moviemakers.

As we sit here in this White House conference, the United States Senate is considering an historic treaty partially banning nuclear tests.

That treaty is an outcome of that scientific revolution—a revolution which, among many other things, set loose the power of the atom, brought a great war to an end, created vast and perilous problems for the very existence of the human race, and brought us to today's debate on the Senate floor.

Our modern world has been shaped by this scientific revolution of the twenties and the thirties. Yet when it was happening, you and I, citizens and statesmen, were conducting our daily affairs in virtual ignorance of the earth-shaking events that were going on around us.

As a result, we were unready for the responsibilities placed on us by the new powers and possibilities science had given us. Even now, as the Senate debate shows, we are struggling to catch up. We are here today to make sure that we never get left behind again.

We are a preparatory conference for the next scientific revolution in the history of man—a conference of officials whose job it is to make sure that society is ready for the discoveries of scientists.

For all around us the signs of a new and momentous revolution are looming larger every day. Those of us working in mental retardation are at the center of that revolution, the advance guard for the wave of the future in science, and thus, in this scientific age, in the life of man.

In 1953, ,Watson, Crick, and Wilkins discovered that hereditary information, the biochemical code which dictates the nature of every living organism, is carried in a chemical known as DNA.

In 1959, Kornberg won the Nobel Prize for synthesizing this chemical.

In 1958, Lederberg shared the Nobel Prize for uncovering some of the basic mechanisms underlying heredity. He is now working in the Kennedy Laboratories of Molecular Medicine, laboratories devoted to the study of mental retardation. He shared that prize with George Beadle, President of the University of Chicago, who recently dedicated the Kennedy Laboratories at the Massachusetts General Hospital.

Dr. Lejeune of France recently won the Kennedy Award for proving that mongolism was characterized by an extra chromosome in the cells, a discovery which offers hope of ultimately controlling that dread human affliction, a discovery which again attacks one of the most intransigent forms of mental retardation.

Donald Glaser, winner of the Nobel Prize in physics, a young and brilliant scientist, announced his intention to switch his field of interest to microbiology, because this field was the challenge of the future. He is now working on mapping the genetic characteristics of bacteria, work which may ultimately shed light on many forms of mental retardation.

A Nobel Prize winner has proclaimed: "Darwin's theory set off the historic debate on man's past. Today, with biology, we mirror his future."

All of this, the new discoveries, the surge of interest, the current of excitement sweeping through the scientific community are the auguries of a new scientific age.

And this revolution, this new knowledge, will have consequences for man more important, more awesome, and more complex than the uncovering of the forces which unleashed the atom and set us on a pathway to the moon.

For we are working to understand, not the universe around us, but the world within us; not the matter which surrounds us, but the nature of our own organism; not the forces which affect life, but life itself.

Over the ancient temple at Delphi was carved the maxim, "Know thyself." For the first time in the more than two thousand years since that command was set forth, science is beginning to open the doors to knowledge of ourselves—to the mechanisms and the stuff of life itself.

In the decades to come, our world, and the world of our children, will be profoundly shaped by what we are now, tentatively, hesitatingly, but surely, beginning to learn. That is why we are here today.

Mental retardation is not one disease. It is the result of a hundred diseases—of genetic structure, chemical imbalance, failures in techniques of learning and training. Wherever scientists are laboring to understand the human mind and the human body, wherever they seek to understand fundamental life processes, their work will have consequences for the millions of mentally retarded.

It is your job to seek out and apply the practical consequences of this new knowledge, to translate theory into techniques and applications which can affect the health of mankind. It was decades before the theoretical discoveries of Einstein could be transformed into the realities of nuclear fission. We cannot afford to wait decades to use the vast potential of our new knowledge to help the sick, relieve the afflicted, and give hope to those threatened with darkness.

Many of you began your work among the retarded when we were still the prisoners of the theories such as that expressed by Dr. Walter Fernald: "The feeble-minded are a parasitic, predatory class, never capable of self-support or managing their own affairs." We have all seen, in the past few years, advances in knowledge and understanding which make these words of only fifty years ago seem like echoes from the remoteness of the Middle Ages.

We have discovered ways to prevent some of the most dread forms of retardation like phenylketonuria, PKU. We have discovered new ways to educate and rehabilitate those who, a few years ago, were condemned to hopeless darkness.

Yet we are only at the beginning. For we will learn more

about retardation in the decade to come than we have learned in the entire history of medicine.

This knowledge, these new discoveries, the painstaking work of the laboratories, will only take on meaning from your work. The retarded will not be helped merely by reactions in a test tube, by papers in a journal, or even by Nobel Prizes.

They can only be helped if you, the workers in every state and community, develop the institutions and the interest, the cures and the concern, the treatments and the techniques, for putting our knowledge practically and immediately to work in the life of the retarded and those threatened with retardation.

Today, and in the days to come, you will examine specific techniques and programs—political, institutional, social, and scientific—designed to accomplish this end.

The opportunities for advance are all around us. Science discovered that the cause of hydrocephalus was a flow of spinal fluid to the brain. But it remained for a private citizen, an engineer, to develop a small valve which could be placed in the neck to control this flow.

We know the cause of PKU, and we know it can be controlled by regulating the diet of infants. But unless you establish testing centers in hospitals in every state this knowledge will be useless and thousands of children will be unnecessarily condemned to an existence as retardates.

A leading authority has estimated that one-third to one-half of all retarded persons could be released from institutions, made relatively self-sufficient, by new techniques of training and rehabilitation. But they will remain in institutions, a burden to society, deprived of basic elements of human dignity, unless we put these techniques to work in our cities and towns and states.

On you and others like you lies the responsibility for this new light now being shed on the nature of man. It is your privilege to be part of an historic surge of new knowledge, to help open up a new life for the retarded, to begin a new journey across the unknown to the land of hope.

4. Vocational Education and the Arts

On October 26, 1956, this talk was given to the first Conference of Large-City Superintendents of Education. Mr. Shriver opened it as President of the Chicago School Board. It was the first time the educational officials of the nation's sixteen largest cities had met together. Out of this meeting developed the Great Cities School Improvement program, financed by the Ford Foundation. The principal topic of this first meeting of superintendents was "Vocational Education."

THERE IS NO USE in building a ten-million-dollar up-to-date school building and then using it as a jail. We must never use our vocational education program as a dumping ground for disciplinary cases. We are trying to educate students, not just trying to give them a vocation. When we use the term "vocational education," therefore, our emphasis should be on the word "education" and not on the word "vocation."

Do we teach our vocational students, even the best of them, very much about the dignity of work? Do we teach that the good workman is willing to sacrifice for his work, just as the good teacher sacrifices for his students, or the patriot sacrifices for his country? Do we give our students any reasons for believing that it is worth while to sacrifice for their work?

I shall never forget an experience I had in Austria, in 1934.

I was with a group of Americans who were living with Austrian families. One afternoon we went to a folk opera performed in the beautiful setting of the Austrian Alps. The composer was a distinguished Austrian known all over Europe. When the performance was concluded, the cast and the composer, our Austrian friends, and the villagers who had made up the audience all gathered together for a coffee break. I found the distinguished composer talking to the local baker—and when I say baker, I don't mean the President of Bond Bread. I mean the man who gets up early in the morning and bakes the bread. They were good friends and respected each other's professional attainments. In this same group were a local policeman and the manager of a small inn. They were talking about opera, and each of them contributed to the conversation. There was no class distinction. This scene comes to my mind frequently when I think of our own failure in this country to achieve a similar respect between peoples of widely varying occupations.

Consider the famous slogan of the Benedictine monks: *"Laborare est orare"*—"To Work Is to Pray"—a slogan seen on monasteries and abbeys throughout the world. Do we attempt to help our vocational education students appreciate the dignity of work which would enable them to believe in their hearts that when they work they are, in effect, praying?

Last night, while you were struggling here with these difficult problems of educational theory and practice, I was enjoying myself at the weekly concert of the Chicago Symphony Orchestra. In the program, I read about some of the great treasures in the possession of the Chicago Symphony. Singled out for special acknowledgment and praise were the five Stradivarius cellos and violins, all built in the eighteenth century, creations of workmanship and craftsmanship the equals of which cannot be made today. My mind recalled the Museum of Modern Art's exhibitions of useful objects, objects of daily living which have an intrinsic beauty of their own. In such exhibitions I have seen typewriters and telephones, knives, forks and spoons, glasses, even a floor mop. How artificial has been the divorce we have created between art and life, between the useful and the artistic! Think of the extraordinary reverence which the Japanese culture has developed for inanimate matter—concern for wood, vegetation, even for paper. How much do we try to teach our vocational education students about the materials with which they work? Do we teach them to appreciate the intrinsic beauty of wood, or of metal, or of cloth? Or do we merely instruct them in the manipulation of these materials?

Western man has been weak, I believe, in this appreciation of materials. But Einstein has killed materialism in science. He taught us that matter is a form of energy. Since we are so partial to scientific explanations, we have accepted his explanation, and now scientific, Western, materialistic man is beginning to respect inanimate nature once again.

Do you remember the hue and cry that arose when the George Washington Bridge was nearing completion over the Hudson River in New York? The magnificent steel columns were bare for everyone to see, but the original plan called for these steel structures to be encased in concrete like most bridges built up to that time. When the contractor started to cover the steel structure, however, public objection was so great that the work was discontinued. Today the intricate and beautiful steelwork in the George Washington Bridge, and in the Golden Gate Bridge, and others, is naked for the human eye to appreciate. Or consider the glass walls of the Lever Building in New York. Or note the contemporary sculptors who use wire, steel, and silver as well as the traditional materials of marble, stone, and bronze. But again I ask, are we teaching our vocational education students anything about this reverence for inanimate matter?

This leads to a similar question: How much do we encourage our students to strive for excellence, for superior performance, for "craftsmanship"? Two weeks ago, I attended the annual meeting of the Board of Governors of the Menninger Foundation, the famous institution for psychiatric care of those suffering from mental illness. One of the developments which struck me most forcibly at that institution was the growing trend among the psychiatrists, who used to rely primarily on psychoanalysis for the cure of patients, to concentrate now on the results to be achieved by music therapy, art therapy, craft therapy, recreational therapy, even religious therapy. These men are grappling with intricate problems involved in "diseases" of the mind. They are finding out that many of their patients can be "cured" by developing in them the desire to create a superior product or to perform well in music, in wood, or in cloth.

We would not be far afield if we tried to develop such an appreciation for outstanding performance on the part of our students. To encourage our students to develop true excellence, we must be willing to separate them on the basis of the quality of their performance, putting some into advanced classes. And since education is an art, and the essence of art includes what the artist omits as well as what he puts in, what courses are we prepared to omit? If merely to impart skills is not the totality of vocational education, what are we doing to awaken intellectual curiosity in our students? What are we doing to stir up a desire for self-education and to teach them how to pursue it after graduation?

It is well to be prepared for life as it is, but it is even better to be prepared to make life better than it is. Vocational education can play a vital role in helping our young people realize that this world can be improved, and that they can play an important part in building a better life for themselves and for their children.

These further remarks on vocational education were given on March 14, 1957, at the dedication of the Dunbar Vocational School.

THE DEDICATION of a vocational school may seem like an unusual occasion to discuss poetry. Poetry is probably the most useless commodity in the world today. No one wants to buy it. Practically no one can make a living composing it.

Yet Paul Laurence Dunbar, for whom this magnificent structure is named, was a poet. He was one of those strange men, useless perhaps to many, but a glory to the Negro people, to our country, and to our civilization. It is significant that in Chicago, industrial capital of the greatest industrial nation in world history, we should be dedicating our newest and best vocational school to the memory of a poet.

In 1895, William Dean Howells, the great literary critic, commented upon Dunbar's poetry in these words:

I permitted myself the imaginative prophecy that the hostilities and prejudices, which had so long constrained his race, were destined to "vanish in the arts"; that these were to be the final proof that God had made of one blood all nations of men. . . . I accepted them as an evidence of the essential unity of the human race, which does not think or feel black in one and white in another, but humanly in all.

This prediction that the hostilities and prejudices against the Negro were destined to "vanish in the arts" has haunted my mind. I believe that Howells was right; that Dunbar Vocational School, large and expensive though it may seem to be, is right; that Chicago is right in naming this school for a poet; and that our program of education in our vocational high schools is right.

The coal miner, who saw only the darkness of his pits, found his children following him into the same work. The textile worker at his loom, or the merchant sailor at sea, passed on to his children the trade he knew because it was all he knew. And in most of the world today, we see this age-old pattern still in operation. In India the caste system imprisons millions within their occupational and cultural group; in Russia no one may change his job or status without government approval; in China men are shackled to their jobs with no hope of liberation.

Two great forces have worked to change this ancient pattern: religion and education; especially liberal education, so named because it liberated man, opened his mind to a full view of society, and gave him light to guide his children into a full participation in the life of mankind.

Dunbar Vocational School provides every student with a firm foundation in these liberal arts—the arts, skills, and interests of free men. Here men and women learn to work at vocations and trades; but they are taught, too, that there is a legitimate connection between the fine arts and the useful arts.

English literature passes before their eyes, and hopefully, into their hearts. Perhaps for the first time in their lives many students here at Dunbar will meet some of the most exciting characters and ideas in the world: Hamlet, speaking to his father's ghost; Shelley's skylark; Keat's Grecian urn, which promises us that "Beauty is truth, truth beauty." Romeo and Juliet, and those lovers in the real world, Elizabeth and Robert Browning: "How do I love thee? Let me count the ways. . . ." The laughing Mark Twain; the simplicity of the Shropshire lad: "When I was one-and-twenty I heard a wise man say, 'Give crowns and pounds and guineas But not your heart away. . . .' "

In music classes, students here at Dunbar learn the "Art of Listening," whether to jazz or symphony. In art, their eyes feast on the colors of Matisse and the depths of Rembrandt.

Dunbar's students are having their ears, eyes, and minds opened, while their hands are trained to create the useful products of contemporary industrial society. This is as it should be. For it is no accident that many of the most beautiful things in America are also the most useful: the Golden Gate Bridge, the jet airplane, the skyscraper office building.

It is no accident either that Chicago was the scene in the United States of the wedding of the artistic with the useful. In Chicago Louis Sullivan first gave artistic expression to the utilitarian skyscraper. Here in our city he and David Adler first explored the skyscraper's true nature in buildings constructed to adorn our boulevards. Miës van der Rohe, who lives here, is now revolutionizing the skyline of America with new buildings which wed the useful to the beautiful more strictly than ever before. In Chicago Frank Lloyd Wright changed the world-wide course of architecture. Sinclair Lewis, James T. Farrell, John Dos Passos, and Theodore Dreiser began the movement in American literature which awakened appreciation for the beauty of plain words.

These men and others like them are responsible in part for our civic awareness today. They have opened our eyes and hearts to the realization that all our surroundings should exemplify the good life, the freedom of liberated men.

Today we see this new type of "Freedom of the City" becoming specific and tangible in our civic determination that there shall be no more "Trumbull Parks"—no more riots based on racial hatred in Chicago. We see it in our new school buildings too, situated, as they should be, in the midst of spacious parks, in surroundings designed to lift the spirit of man.

Our "days are never days of ease," wrote Paul Laurence Dunbar. And, in the words of the poet whose memory we honor tonight:

> Sometimes the sun, unkindly hot,
> My garden makes a desert spot;

Sometimes a blight upon the tree
Takes all my fruit away from me;
And then with throes of bitter pain
    Rebellious passions rise and swell;
But—life is more than fruit or grain,
    And so I sing, and all is well.*

* From "The Poet and His Song" in *The Complete Poems of Paul Laurence Dunbar*. Reprinted by permission of Dodd, Mead & Company, Inc.

5. Aims of Education

On October 7, 1958, this talk was given to the Illinois Association of Secondary School Principals Convention, held at the University of Illinois.

Educators complain that everyone wants to get into *their* act. Yet people do have a right to criticize, to suggest, to urge changes. Public schools are public business, but popular intervention can go too far. Everybody's opinion is not equally good in determining what our schools should teach.

Plato wrote these words in the *Protagoras*:

When the matter in hand relates to buildings, the builders are summoned as advisers; when the question is one of ship-building, then the ship-wrights; . . . and if some person offers advice who is not supposed to have any skill in the art, even if he is good looking, and rich and noble, they will not listen to him, but laugh and hoot at him, until either he is clamoured down and retires of himself; or if he persist, he is dragged away or put out by the constables.

But that was two thousand years ago. Now we are advised in elementary and high school education to conduct a public opinion poll to determine what the people in an area think they need. This way the people would determine what ought to be taught, and the educators how to teach it. The community next door using the same procedure may, of course, develop

184

a different set of goals. But both sets of goals would be, by this definition of educational democracy, equally good and acceptable.

Pittsburgh, for example, might develop goals which emphasize metallurgy. Detroit would emphasize industrial design; Los Angeles, the movie industry. To me, this is all nonsense.

Not long ago I was privileged to tour the Far East and to study the educational systems there. Upon my return I urged increased study of other cultures and civilizations and languages. But I was being taken in by one of the most popular doctrines in American education—the doctrine of needs. Here is how the argument runs: Russia is ahead in space technology; therefore we need more science study. Automobile accidents are up; therefore we need more driver education. Divorce rates are up; therefore we need more courses in marriage and the family.

These may all be important subjects. But the basic question is: How do we specify what is to be taught? Everyone will agree that education ought to take care of a person's needs, just as we are all for virtue and the common good. The real issue is: Which needs are most important and how do we discover them?

A hundred years ago nearly every young person needed to be able to recognize when a horse was going lame. Today he needs to know when a tire is about to go flat. Tomorrow he will have to know about jet engines. There are, in short, practical needs which are determined by time and place.

But does a young person in a remote North Dakota town have a practical need to read Russian novelists or the French writer Albert Camus? Does he have a need to know advanced logic and mathematics or foreign languages?

In some communities these may not be regarded as practical needs. But there are needs which are basic to humanity, irrespective of time, place, or culture: mastering language, enjoying music, performing in an art. If these needs, basic to all human beings, are satisfied, then the whole pattern of a student's desires will be different. True education will have created needs where none existed before.

Instead of the doctrine of community needs, may I suggest that the test of good education is whether it will make people want to do, and enjoy, and contemplate the things most worthy of them, whether it opens new vistas for the mind and the soul.

If the citizenry, the public, should not determine the aims of education, who should? You, the educational leaders of Illinois. You should do this job because in a very real sense you are best qualified to do it. You as educators know, or should know, both the timeless, basic needs of man and his "practical," transient needs as an individual in a particular community.

The real problem is: How can these "practical" needs of a particular time and community be covered in our program of studies along with the essential needs of all human beings at all times in all places? Let us begin by agreeing that in educating a young person we are concerned with him, first, as a human being, second, as a social being, and only third as a specialist, in his vocation as an economic being.

This order of priorities postulates that a good man is more important than a good citizen, and that both these qualities are more important than a man's profession or specialty. Only in a totalitarian society can you have a bad man who is also a good citizen. A bad man cannot be a good citizen in a democracy. Even if he is the most "academically talented" man in the country, he is a liability and a misfit. Furthermore, a society of bad citizens would be hell to live in, even if the hourly productivity of each were the highest in the world. Good men and good citizens, I should add, are the kind of human beings who can make intelligent choices about their vocations, their specialties.

Then the first factor to be taken into account in determining the aims of an educational program is not the immediate and local community, but the great human community extending through time and space. The real objective of education is to induct high school students into the community of saints and scholars, philosophers and poets, scientists and statesmen, to help them enjoy and appreciate the works of Shakespeare, Goethe, Mark Twain, Lincoln, Jefferson, T. S. Eliot, Einstein and Mahatma Gandhi. I deny that 80 percent of our high school students are incapable of appreciating or desiring to know about the work and thought of these great men. The liberal arts underlying our belief in science, democracy, human dignity, and freedom are subjects that have a permanent place in the history of Western education. They belong in the secondary school curriculum whether the community raises corn or skyscrapers, is urban or rural, whether the students are "academically gifted" or not.

We parents and citizens do not want to adjust our children to a local culture; we want to emancipate them and help them rise above it, to soar to the heights of human achievement. Education is the greatest means for providing new ideas, for arousing new needs, for opening up new opportunities. This is the most important function of education, and should be extended to all people.

Our schools, even our vocational schools, should not be factories producing specialized workers for a hungry industrial machine. They should not be institutions which seek to give a man a trade and then imprison him within it. That was the attitude in the old days, when knowledge of the liberal arts was restricted to the man who was liberated and the "servile arts" were the destiny of the lower classes. Education has worked for two thousand years to change this ancient pattern.

Today it should be our aim to extend this education universally. It is not our purpose to prepare students only for induction into the existing communities of Pittsburgh, Chicago, or Little Rock. On the contrary, it is our purpose, the purpose of true education, to enfranchise man into the great, human community of free men and free spirits, of all times and all places.

6. Education for the Future

On July 9, 1957, this proposal that American high schools study the seven great world cultures was made to the Conference on School Administration and Educational Leadership, at Northwestern University.

WHAT ABOUT EDUCATION for the more distant future—the future world of the twenty-first century, now only forty-three years away?

The great issue in these years to come is: How can all of us of different nations and different cultures live together in peace? The world's population is growing rapidly. The geographic size of the world, figuratively speaking, is shrinking. Chicago in 1960 will be only one and a half hours from New York City, six hours from London or Cairo. In 1970 New York City will probably be closer in time to Chicago than Waukegan is today.

Under these circumstances, if anyone believes that we in the Chicago of the future will be able to dismiss the problems of India, Africa, or Asia as "foreign affairs" conducted solely by the Secretary of State, he is living in a fool's paradise. We shall be living in a world where Bangkok is as close as Boston is to Dallas. In that world I suggest we shall need more than bombs or radar defense nets. We shall need *understanding* of foreign peoples, cultures, and political traditions—understanding of a type we cannot hope to achieve solely by studying English literature, American history, or democratic principles of life and government. We shall need to know our own history and culture, but we shall have to know other cultures, too. There is an old adage: "He who knows only one language doesn't even know that one well." Tonight I suggest: He who knows only one culture doesn't even know that one culture well.

Instead of concentrating almost entirely on teaching Anglo-Saxon culture in our high schools, I suggest we offer courses in the seven great world cultures, six of which are still living and vying with each other. The cultures for us to study are: the Moslem, the Hindu or Indian, the Chinese or Japanese, the African, the Hebrew-Christian, and, by way of background and perspective, the classical culture of Greece and Rome.

Today in our Chicago public schools we conduct exchange programs between our teachers and teachers from England, Puerto Rico, and elsewhere. I suggest this program can be greatly expanded with beneficial results. The Fulbright Scholarship program is successful at the graduate and professional level. Why not a teacher exchange program of comparable magnitude, but let Indian, Chinese, or Hebrew scholars come here to teach us about *their* cultures as well as to learn about *ours*? In fact, we could, if need be, teach Hebrew and Christian culture without importing any teachers.

Is there room and time in the high school curriculum for this additional work? I believe there is. If there isn't, I think room will have to be made, not by eliminating studies now required, but by speeding up the pace of high school education.

The French *lycée*, the German *Hochschule*, and the English public school have long since proved that more can be learned by age seventeen than we ask of young Americans. I think, too, that many of our smartest students get bored by the pedestrian pace of the average high school. I believe they will welcome an exciting addition to the curriculum. We can also teach these world cultures in special summer schools. This year in Chicago we have 27,000 pupils in free, voluntary, summer school classes.

Let us expand the intellectual horizons of our students to enable them to become leaders of world society, men and women distinguished by their understanding of and consequent love for all mankind whatever the color of skin, the sound of language, the background of mind.

All through the ages we see the creative process of re-education out of which a new humanity is born. Today East and West live cut off from each other through ignorance, not intent. We must build bridges of understanding across this abyss of ignorance. Only in this way can we look forward to world peace.

7. A Case for College Dropouts

On June 7, 1964, at Wesleyan University, Sargent Shriver made a case for a special kind of college dropout.

Most GRADUATES OF AMERICAN COLLEGES and universities today have been involved in an educational marathon. For sixteen continuous years or more you graduates of '64 have been in a lockstep of doing lessons, studying, cramming, writing term papers. Now over 80 percent of you are marching on to graduate school.

But you may notice a number of your classmates who are missing. They are the 35 percent who dropped out of this class. They are the ones who decided that it just was not worth the effort, or that they were not getting out of it what they had hoped to get, or they were not putting into it what they should.

They became dropouts—college dropouts—and that is a national problem that has not been given the attention it needs. Much is written and studied and discussed about high school dropouts, but the college dropout represents an even more serious loss of potential brainpower.

Less than 60 percent of the students who enroll in United States colleges ever graduate, and half of these dropouts quit by the end of two years. Recently the Office of Education reported that male students drop out mainly because of "lack of interest in studies."

It is too easy, especially in an assembly of graduates, to feel superior and forget the ones who didn't "make it," who quit on education in midstream. The records show that these dropouts were not all weak students. Thirty-two percent of them were in the top fifth of their high school graduating class.

What was the problem? One of the problems, perhaps, was that the decision to go to college, the choice of a major field of study, and the determination to see it through to the end are made usually by young people who have had little contact with the "real" world. College is academic to them. For them, college is a staging area, not a battlefield. Most students entering college have never had to make a major decision. It is difficult, they find, to decide whether to spend the rest of your life being a lawyer, or an engineer, or a social scientist, or a history teacher. And once you have made a choice, nothing can discourage interest in a subject faster than having to master it. Many college students feel they are learning in a vacuum.

Suppose there were a moratorium at some point—a moratorium on formal education. As far back as 1950, Dr. Eric Erickson, the noted psychoanalyst, suggested the idea of such a moratorium in a White House Conference on Youth. He saw it as a period away from the classroom in which a youth could "find himself," find out what he really wanted.

Paul Goodman, the distinguished novelist and social critic, picked up the theme again in a recent article. "Suppose," Goodman says,

that half a dozen of the most prestigious liberal arts colleges—say Amherst, Swarthmore, Wesleyan, Carleton, etc.—would announce that, beginning in 1966, they required for admission a two-year period, after high school, spent in some maturing activity—for example, working for a living, community service such as the

Northern Student Movement, or the Peace Corps, work camp, Army, a satisfactory course of travel.

The purpose of this, Goodman writes, would be "to get students with enough life-experience to be educable on the college level." Goodman sees "a desperate need" for such "breaks and return points." Otherwise, he says, "the schooling inevitably becomes spirit-breaking regimentation."

The people who conduct the training programs in the Peace Corps know that Goodman is right. We noticed one thing almost immediately in our training programs: there was an overwhelming eagerness by the trainees to get out and "do" rather than to sit and listen. Many of them were suffering from what might be called "campus fatigue."

Probably, that's not an unfamiliar phrase in this gathering. Many college students by the end of their sophomore year are mentally "burned out." Often they have been pushed, from infancy onward, to get high grades, to get into the "good" prep schools, to get into the "good colleges." By the second year of college they are high on brainwork, but rather low on human experience.

The young men and women we get in the Peace Corps—80 percent college graduates—are still in search of "real life," in search of reality. In a sense they are fugitives from the groves of academe; they want some graduate "experience in the world." Another thing about these Volunteers: when they enter the Peace Corps many of them are uncertain about their major fields of academic study. Then they go overseas for two years, get more experience, more responsibility, more personal stress, than they have ever known before. And when they come home, many of them suddenly have switched their majors. Engineers turn into psychologists, agriculturalists to anthropologists, business majors to history teachers, psychology majors to students of international affairs.

These are not people returning from a vacation abroad, or from mere study abroad. These are veterans of two full years of trying situations and strenuous circumstances. These are people who now know the interiors, the folkways, and some of the languages of the world's civilizations—people whose sense of purpose, whose aims, whose articles of faith have been tempered under fire, who have encountered reality on its own terms, who have finally discovered the world beyond college.

What happened as a result of this journey into reality? Did our Peace Corps volunteers not only change their interest but revolt against education itself? They did not. When the first 545 Volunteers returned to the United States, nearly half of them resumed their academic education, most of them at the graduate level. Ninety-nine of them won assistantships, fellowships, or scholarships. The reality they encountered in the field had not been left behind. The Volunteers brought it to the classroom with them.

Gray Cowan, Director of Columbia University's African Studies Program, says, "They are head and shoulders above the rest of the students in the program. Their higher degree of motivation and greater insight result in a superior academic performance. The more of these returning Volunteers we can get, the better."

The Peace Corps, of course, didn't invent reality. Nor was it the first to reveal what the experience of reality can bring to the classroom. College teachers who taught the two million World War II GI veterans say these men were their best students. They were men with serious questions, men who were not merely interested in exams and marks, but *concerned* about the relationship between their studies and the problems of their own lives, and the great problems of the world.

This seems to be the quality also of our Peace Corps Volunteers who are returning to school. Many are holders of bachelor's degrees who decided to take two years of service as an interval between college and graduate school. Many are undergraduate students on a two-year leave of absence. As a matter of fact, one out of every seven men and women serving in the Peace Corps is, in one sense, a college dropout. Most of these plan to return to college when they complete their Peace Corps service. It is safe to say, though, having stretched out their education for at least two years, that they will stretch it out for the rest of their lives. They are the students who will become those permanently self-educating citizens colleges hope to produce.

Take Mike Glatte, a Volunteer in Ethiopia. He was a dropout from the University of California. He did not get beyond the second year of college. Yet Mike did so well in Peace Corps training that the Ethiopian Government asked for him, even though he didn't meet their requirement of a college degree. In Ethiopia Mike was sent to a run-down slum school for all-Moslem children in Asmara, a school which had never had a foreign teacher. Mike turned out to be an excellent and dedicated teacher. He learned the language. He organized a school library and various clubs. He raised money in the local community, and from the United States, to build new classrooms. He proved to be a leader. The Ethiopian Government wanted him to stay on after his two years. He had done so well the Peace Corps offered him a job at $7,500 per annum. But he turned down all offers in order to go back and finish college.

Take Peter Dybwad, who graduated from Wesleyan in 1961. He was certainly no college dropout. But he turned down both Harvard and Yale Law Schools to join the Peace Corps in Ghana. He was in our first group to go overseas. He taught history in the Akim-Oda high school. When his principal was away he was elected acting principal of the school by the other teachers (all but one were Ghanaians). Now Peter is home and back in school (Yale Law School). This is what he says about his experience in the Peace Corps: "I would rather have a penniless and wretched old age after a full and varied life, than a 'secure' old age paid for by a careful and safe career."

Like the returning GI's, these Volunteers are now not merely interested, but concerned. They are not merely curious; they care. They care about education of the poor in Nyasaland, prevention of disease in Malaysia, agricultural advancement for Pakistan, community action for rural villages in Peru.

And they care about the same problems among the thirty million rural and urban poor in this country. Eighty-two percent of the returned Peace Corps Volunteers have already declared a strong interest in working in President Johnson's War on Poverty, in training the unskilled, teaching the illiterate, helping the mentally retarded and the aged, supervising recreation for fatherless children.

Their dedication, their zeal, their sense of commitment is the sort of influence, the sort of climate, we need to create on our campuses in America: a climate of concern. Yet today most college students enroll in college with their eye on the degree that awaits them at the end, and the job, financial success, and social position that the degree promises to bring.

Does your degree mean no more than this to you? Is it only a letter of reference for a high-paying job? What is education for, if not to make better, more learned people who will make a better world?

What has all this to do with college dropouts? The college dropout problem does not have to be a problem at all. It can be a plus instead of a minus, a plus for the student who drops out, a plus for America, a plus for the world.

In other words, if the college sophomore wants to drop out, let him! Let the bored, or confused, or "burned-out" undergraduate have a short, meaningful interlude, a journey to reality, for a year, or even two years, so that he may come back revitalized, committed, concerned enough to finish both college and graduate school. And let these interludes be periods of service, whether in the Peace Corps or the poverty program, with the American Friends or the Papal Volunteers or any other service involving the reality of human needs.

These short periods of service could inspire young men and women toward whole lives of service, and nothing short of whole lives of service will be required of Americans in the coming decades.

The idea of these "dropout" periods is already gaining support, even in academic circles. Our Peace Corps Director in Nigeria, William Saltonstall, used to be Headmaster of Exeter. He urged President Pusey of Harvard not to accept any graduate of Exeter who had not spent a year away from school. He insisted that high school graduates need to learn about other realities in the world besides exams and grades, other people in the world besides their schoolmates and families.

President Harrington of the University of Wisconsin has urged two-year leaves for undergraduates, beginning in either their sophomore or junior years. For two years' service in some work-study capacity he proposes that students receive one year's undergraduate credit.

Here at Wesleyan, many of you have done very well as undergraduates in part-time projects in Middletown. When Dean Barlow assessed student involvement at the end of the first semester, he found eighty-eight undergraduates involved in the program for mental patients at the Connecticut Valley Hospital; sixty who had taught in the Negro Tutoring Program; sixteen working with church youth groups; nineteen with the Boy Scouts; twenty-seven with the YMCA; and thirteen actively participating in the local NAACP.

All of this is commendable, but does it mean you have disposed of your obligation to give service? If that is so, then all it does is to confirm the traditional notion of service which must now be abandoned—the old idea that service is a spare-time activity, basically unrelated to what one *really* does in life.

Service is not a short-term debt. It's a lifetime investment.

Twelve members of this Wesleyan Class of 1964 have applied to the Peace Corps. But the majority of you have made another kind of commitment, to graduate school, professional school, or both. Are you committed for life? Are you going on to graduate school to prepare for involvement in the issues of our time? Are you preparing to be a professional, in the highest sense of the word? Or are you going simply to avoid involvement, to avoid the draft or, worse still, because you have nothing better to do?

Fifteen centuries ago, St. Augustine wrote: "Those that sit at rest while others take pains are tender turtles, and buy their quiet with disgrace."

There is no room in the twentieth-century Ark for tender turtles. Make your decision in favor of taking pains, in favor of involvement, in favor of commitment; create a climate of concern in America.

At the end of James Joyce's *Portrait of the Artist as a Young Man,* the youthful hero, Stephen Daedalus, turns away from the narrow provincialism of his native Dublin, and delivers this valedictory:

"I go to encounter for the millionth time the reality of experience . . . to forge in the smithy of my soul the uncreated conscience of my race."

The American conscience was created by the founders of this country. But America still needs blacksmiths. It needs men —and women—who in the smithy of their souls can forge a link to that conscience. It needs men—and women—who are ready to encounter reality, and make it a happier reality for men and women everywhere.

VII

THE SOUL

OF

OUR NATION

"It is not by the sword that deliverance comes
to nations; the sword cannot breed peace, it can only
impose terms of peace. The forces that are to renew
the earth must proceed from within, from the spirit."
—JACQUES MARITAIN

Franklin Roosevelt made much of this point when, speaking of
the 1920's, he said that "Lulled by material prosperity, the soul
of our nation has gone through eight gray years." From various
angles and points in time, the "soul of our nation" is the subject under discussion in this part. Franklin Roosevelt's reference is in contrast to Joseph Stalin's scornful question to a
leader of India: "What is this thing called 'soul' ? " The Indian
replied: "That which you have not got."

This is the contrast which always exists between those who
believe in the dignity and destiny of every human being and
those who believe only in things and theories. The soul is that
element which this nation must never lose.

1. Inheritors of an Age

May 30, 1964, was the first Memorial Day after the death of Eleanor Roosevelt. On that day, at the invitation of the Roosevelt family, Sargent Shriver spoke at Hyde Park as part of the annual Roosevelt memorial service.

"IN ALL THE YEARS of my husband's public life," said Eleanor Roosevelt, "I never once heard him make a remark which indicated that any crisis could not be solved."

This Memorial Day you have done me the honor of asking me to speak at the lifelong home and final resting place of two people whose lives were a testament to the creative power of man to solve his own problems. The Roosevelts were the finest examples of the nation which they loved and led. Through their work the United States passed successfully through the most troubled and dangerous period of its history into an era, not less troubled, but with a shape and challenge which is a product of their triumph.

We have before us difficulties as fresh and as grave as those that challenged Franklin Roosevelt. But the nature of those difficulties and our capacity to deal with them have been profoundly influenced by his life and his work.

I come here today not as a participant in the age of Roosevelt, but as an inheritor of that age. He was the principal architect of our America.

It is said that Roosevelt's task was easier because he took office at a time of great national crisis. The normal processes of political debate were suspended, opposition had been submerged by the flood of national misery, and everyone turned to him expectantly for leadership. This created a great opportunity, but it also magnified the dangers of failure.

The Preamble to the Constitution lists among the objectives of the American people to "establish justice, insure domestic tranquillity, provide for the common defense, promote the general welfare, and secure the blessings of liberty to ourselves and our posterity." In our entire history no leader was truer to that mandate than Franklin Roosevelt.

Roosevelt laid the foundations of today's affluent society, and established the principle that the nation was responsible for the general welfare of all its citizens. Although poverty and injustice remain, we have today, for the first time, the legal and material resources to end them.

In our dealings with the world, he thrust America, almost against its will, into the center of the world arena. He strengthened us to defeat our most brutal and powerful enemies and destroyed the isolationism and parochial outlook which had kept the United States from assuming its responsibilities as part of a greater world community.

Because of him, for the first time in our history the issue is not whether we will have the strength to deal with our problems, but whether we have the courage and determination to use that strength; not whether we have the resources, but whether we choose to use those resources for the world's welfare; not whether we can, but whether we will.

Today's central issue is a moral issue: the issue of commitment. Largely because of Roosevelt we are the first nation in history with the strength to solve its own problems. If we fail, it will be a failure of commitment.

We can eliminate unemployment and poverty in this country. We can ensure some measure of security against the ravages of disease and old age. We can enable the Negro to become simply and fully an American. We can harness and use science for the welfare of our people. We can work for a world in which almost three billion underprivileged people will be our colleagues in progress.

This is not said lightly. These are not easy problems. I have seen the face of poverty and idleness in the mines of West Virginia. I have come face to face with racial hatred on the South Side of Chicago: Catholics stoning fellow Catholics on the steps of a church because they were black. In the last few years, I have traveled five hundred thousand miles around the world seeing at first hand the deep barriers of culture, belief, prejudice, and superstition which divide us from our fellow man.

But I have also seen the power of commitment, the individual commitment of thousands of Peace Corps Volunteers doing more than any of us can realize to refashion our relationships to the rest of the world. The Peace Corps is proof that deeply committed individuals can have a profound impact on the most difficult and intransigent of problems. Further proof is found in the civil rights movement. To the commitment of those in the front lines of the struggle must be added that of homeowners joining to break down housing ghettos, of businessmen joining to bring about desegregation, of religious leaders actively recruiting Negro members for their congregation.

What can we do about it? you ask. There is much you can do. For the need is not merely for laws or Presidential action, but for the self-organization of society on a large scale to solve the problems. The proof of this is in the North—in Chicago and New York and Washington—where our books are full of good laws and regulations, but where hypocrisy and racial hatred and the apathy of decent citizens have made a mockery of American justice and equal opportunity.

We must now show that we have the personal commitment to use our wealth and strength in the construction of a good society at home and throughout the world.

2. The Meeting of Church and State

This commencement address was given on June 12, 1963, at Fordham University.

"UT UNUM SINT," John XXIII said in his last days. "That we may all be one."

This phrase, better than any other, sums up his life and work. He was a "Pope of Reconciliation"—reconciliation between East and West, Catholics and non-Catholics, the powerful and the weak, poor nations and wealthy ones. "All men," he wrote in *Pacem in Terris,* "are equal in their natural dignity." He recognized the presence of conflict, of deep differences of belief and desire; but he believed that in the long run the divine spark which unites men would prove stronger than the forces which divide.

It is amazing to me that this humble man, granted only a few years among us as Pope, the author of only a few encyclicals, the convener of only one half-finished council, the host to distinguished but relatively few visitors from differing nations and creeds, could have had such a profound impact on the thinking of the entire world. Through him the doors of the Church were opened onto the modern world, revealing, across those ancient casements, the prospects of a world in which the knowledge, the hopes, and the suspicions of modern man would be reconciled and elevated by the most enduring of our religious and spiritual beliefs. His Pontificate marks a turning point from which there can be no retreat.

Let me focus his principle of reconciliation on one of the most troublesome questions of our society: the relationship of Church and State. Here, too, historic dogmas must come to terms with the realities of today's life.

I speak to you not as a philosopher or theologian or even as a political scientist. For I am none of these. I am only a public servant. But my work has taken me to thirty countries. It has enabled me to send young Americans of every religious persuasion to almost fifty countries of mixed beliefs. I have seen firsthand how basic spiritual beliefs and deeds can shatter barriers of politics and creed.

Therein lies the genius of John XXIII. He recognized that mankind's greatest yearning is for an end to division and conflict. He reached out and touched our common heart. In this, among the great world leaders, he was the first modern man.

There was a time in the West when Christ's admonition to keep distinct our obligations to God and Caesar was neglected; when religion fought for control of the State, and the State for control of religion; when differences of belief were fought out on the battlefield. There was a time, too, when the poor and oppressed found that the Church was aligned with the rich and the powerful against them.

From this flowed the erection of legal barriers between Church and State and the rise of anticlericalism.

We must remember that our own First Amendment has as its primary purpose, not only the protection of the State against religion, but the protection of religion against the State. Jefferson wrote: "I consider the Government of the United States as interdicted by the Constitution from intermeddling with religious institutions, their doctrines, disciplines or exercises . . . Civil powers alone have been given to the President of the United States and no authority to direct the religious exercises of his constituents."

And one hundred twenty-five years later the Supreme Court has written: "If there is any fixed star in our Constitutional constellation, it is that no official, high or petty, can prescribe what shall be orthodox in politics, nationalism, religion or other matters of opinion."

Today most of the old sources of conflict have disappeared from our society. The religious wars have ended; churches are secure from State domination; and the State has given up efforts to prescribe a belief which all men must follow on pain of punishment or disability. We no longer burn witches or exile nonbelievers. And under the great experiment of religious liberty both Church and State have flourished.

In fact, the settling of these ancient divisions is the touch-stone of modern political life, the mark of the modern state. And no one understood better than Pope John that these old disputes had been drained of their content. He refused to make war on the past. Nations like the Soviet Union with their officially prescribed creeds are, indeed, living in the past. They have not yet caught up with the spirit of the age and, until they do, can lay little claim to being modern nations.

Unfortunately, there are still those who view the separation of Church and State as conducive to hostility, conflict, and suspicion. To all efforts at fruitful cooperation they return the answer, "They shall not pass." They live with fears as outdated as the rack and inquisition which helped produce them.

It was an outstanding Jew, Justice Felix Frankfurter, who helped give the answer. "Religion is outside the sphere of political government," he wrote, "but this does not mean that all matters on which religious organizations . . . may pronounce are outside the sphere of Government. . . . Much that is the concern of temporal authority affects the spiritual interests of men."

And it was my deputy, Bill Moyers, a Southern Baptist, trained as a minister of his church, who suggested that I reaffirm to you today his belief as well as mine that separation of Church and State does not mean the divorce of spiritual values from secular affairs.

Separation of Church and State meant one thing when government and religion were at cross purposes. It means something different when they have common purposes. Today they have such common purpose in "social progress." The great social questions—war and peace, civil rights, education, the elimination of poverty at home and abroad—are all, at bottom, moral questions. They reflect spiritual values. They are the concern of religion and government; they are the concern of millions who perceive no difference, in this regard, between their beliefs and their social obligations.

This principle, the identity of private morality and public conscience, is as deeply rooted in our tradition and Constitution as the principle of legal separation. Washington, in his First Inaugural, said that the roots of national policy lay in private morality. De Tocqueville observed that American democracy was uniquely founded on morality. Lincoln proclaimed as a national faith that "right makes might."

Those who would read the Constitution as erecting a wall of hostility and distrust between Church and State neglect this aspect of our tradition. They are blind to the spiritual mainstream of American life. Legal separation is an important principle. Equally important is the need for cooperation and common effort in attacking social problems. For the State to deprive itself of the support of religious belief and organization is to enter the battle for social justice without our strongest weapon: the spiritual beliefs from which social action springs. And without the cooperation of Church and State, of belief and power, our efforts will be doomed to failure.

The Peace Corps is an example of the need for spiritual values in the work of government. And its work is, in the deepest sense, the work of reconciliation. It is a model of that fellow-ship aimed at construction of a united world community to which John XXIII devoted his Pontificate.

The first two Volunteers to be killed on the job were a Jew and a Protestant. They died in a Catholic country and the Bishop who consecrated their death called them "martyrs." *El Tiempo,* the principal newspaper of Bogotá, editorialized:

They were the first to fulfill the Rite of Blood which united them [with Colombians] in an indissoluble tie. . . . Their bodies . . . have fallen with those of our fellow countrymen. The sacrifice of blood is thus consummated. Two races were forged together in this dramatic accident. That this be not in vain, is the ardent hope of millions of human beings.

We have Peace Corps Volunteers of all faiths teaching in more than one hundred Catholic Mission schools abroad. We have Volunteers of all faiths teaching in more than one hundred Protestant Mission schools. We have Volunteers of all faiths teaching in Buddhist schools. And there has not been one in-stance of racial or religious clash, not one instance in which belief has interfered with the day's work. Strong moral purpose has enhanced, not hampered, the progress of the Peace Corps.

Yet at every step of the way we were met with the warnings of the timid. "Don't send Negroes to Africa," we were warned, "the Africans will think you are condescending." "You can't send Jews to Tunisia and Morocco." "You can't send Protestants to the Catholic country of Colombia." "You can't send Puerto Ricans to Latin America because 'they' look on Puerto Rico as an American colony." We refused to heed any of these warnings. And they all proved untrue—the folklore of "experts" who had never got to the level of the people.

The fact is that compassion and service can dissolve obstacles of race or belief anywhere in the world. People are hungry for contact, for fellowship, for the breaking down of barriers.

Hopefully, the Peace Corps is both a symbol and a forerunner of a genuine world-wide effort among people of different nations, different religions, and different races to establish an ecumenical community among men.

But the growth of understanding between Church and State, the infusion of spiritual values into secular affairs, the breaking down of barriers between nations and peoples, the modernity of Pope John, the success of the Peace Corps, do not represent final victories. They represent a challenge and an obligation.

In *Mater et Magistra* Pope John wrote that to meet the great social problems of the world "It is necessary to arouse a sense of responsibility in individuals and especially among those more blessed with the world's goods." Every one of you who are graduating today are among those blessed with the world's goods. It is you that Pope John meant.

The senseless, terrible murder of integrationist leader Medgar Evers in Jackson, Mississippi, proves again the depth of our moral blindness on race relations. How many of us are giving time or money to the solution of this moral crisis of our national life? Much more must be done by every one of us.

John XXIII gave his life to the service of God and of all his fellow men, regardless of race, creed, or nationality.

It was in that spirit—that all may be one: *"Ut unum sint"*— that he said, "To serve God is to rule."

3. The Challenge of a Communist Poet

*This talk at the San Diego State College Convocation on Octo-
ber 7, 1963, is one of a number of times Sargent Shriver discussed the Russian poet Yevtushenko's challenging book,*
A Precocious Autobiography.

I AM HAPPY to be in "the Peace Corps state." California has
produced more than 700 of the 5,500 Volunteers now at work
overseas. And California colleges have trained more of our
Volunteers than any other state. This is the kind of response
we hoped to produce when we printed our first information
poster with the question: "What in the World Are You Doing?"

To appreciate the need for this American response, you
should listen to the ideas of one of Russia's foremost poets,
Yevgeny Yevtushenko. He is thirty years old. His message has
already stirred millions of young Russians. He speaks words
you do not expect to hear from a Communist. They represent
the beginning of a profound revolution within Communism,
a revolution far more disturbing to the West, because it challenges our grand assumption that we and we alone are champ-
ions of the human spirit and defenders of human values,
that we alone have plumbed the nature of man and understood his most urgent yearnings.

Listen to Yevtushenko:

It is the more fortunate nations, those favored by their geographical position and historical circumstances, that today show a grosser spirit and a weaker hold on moral principles. Nor would I call those nations happy, despite all the signs of their prosperity. Never has the Biblical saying, "Man does not live by bread alone," had such a ring of truth as it does today.

Man has a need to dream. However prosperous, a man will always be dissatisfied if he has no high ideal. And whatever devices he may use to conceal his dissatisfaction even from himself, these will only make him feel more dissatisfied. But even if the rich feel burdened by the lack of an ideal, to those who suffer real deprivation an ideal is a first necessity of life. Where there is plenty of bread and a shortage of ideals, bread is no substitute for an ideal. But where bread is short, ideals are bread.

Yevtushenko's idealism refutes the dogmatists in America who argue that Communist ideals are empty. They say the march of Soviet power conceals the bankruptcy of their ideology. They say that the Soviets are moved by power, not by poetry. But this year fourteen thousand Russians filled the Moscow Sports Palace to hear Yevtushenko recite his poetry. And twenty thousand wrote in praise when one poem came off the presses—a response yet to be accorded any single work of an American writer.

Yevtushenko has something to say about his people's idealism:

We have paid for ideals with so much blood and torment that the cost itself has endeared it and made it more precious to us, as a child born in pain is more precious to its mother.

You may say, "But doesn't it occur to you that Communism itself may be a false ideal?" If the reader believes in God, I will ask him, "Can you equate the substance of the Christian religion with the swindlers who used to make a handsome profit by selling indulgences, with the inquisitors, the priests who got rich at their parishioners' expense, or parishioners who pray piously in church and double-deal outside its walls?" Neither can I, a believing Communist, equate the essence of my religion with the crooks who climb on its bandwagon, with its inquisitors, its crafty, avaricious priests, or its double-dealing, double-faced parishioners.

For me, a Communist is not merely someone who belongs to the organization and pays his dues. A Communist is a man who puts the people's interests above his own.

Do we see the significance of what he is saying? And the significance of the freedom he has today to say these things? For years, Communism has been its own worst enemy. The very inhumanity of Communist practice repelled the humanity its ideology was trying to win. No matter how poorly practiced, Western ideals stood out in sharp contrast to the fundamental indifference of Communism to human values.

But now, if Yevtushenko is right, Communism is undergoing a revolution. And as it does, a far greater gauntlet will be flung at the West than the specter of Soviet missiles and nuclear submarines: the gauntlet of Communist ideas. He is trying to get his fellow Communists to see that the decisive weapon in an era of nuclear stalemate is not a nation's sword but its spirit.

Russia may not be ready for Yevtushenko. Already he has been censured by Khrushchev himself. But so long as Yevtushenko continues to challenge his own country he will be a challenge to us. In calling for the "purification" of Communism, he is saying that Western society is empty, stripped of ideas, an aimless wasteland.

The Soviet Union is not withdrawing from its vision of a new world order dominated by one political system: Communism. But, if Yevtushenko's generation prevails, that system will be given a spiritual content with the power to draw humanity to its cause.

We have our vision, too, of a world of liberty under law, of an open society for all men. Are we committed to making that vision a reality?

4. Our Dream Government of the Future

This May 7, 1956, talk was given to high school student leaders at the YMCA's Youth Citizenship Meeting in Chicago.

Is ANYONE TALKING OR WRITING or working on the "Dream Government of the Future"? This year at the 1956 Automobile Show the displays which attracted the most attention were the Dream Cars of the Future. Last week a "Dream Train of the Future"—the Aerotrain—was put into experimental operation between Chicago and Detroit. But what about our government?

Will our government be the same in the year 2000 as it is to-day? Are we opposed to all change in government? Is it subversive to suggest or even discuss changes in government?

Plato in ancient Greece wrote his Utopia, *The Republic,* without losing his standing as a loyal Athenian. Sir Thomas More wrote his celebrated *Utopia* in sixteenth-century England when he was Lord High Chancellor of the King's Realm, the highest judicial office in England.

What about our Utopia?

Is George Orwell's book, *1984,* the symbol of our Utopia, our world of the future, filled with secret police, concentration camps, factories for rewriting history? Or will our Utopia be the fulfillment of the Constitution?

In the United States we used to have great hopes, even

dreams. Thomas Paine, in the middle of our Revolution, wrote *Common Sense*, a book filled with hopes and dreams for an equalitarian society. Abraham Lincoln wrote of "government of the people, by the people, and for the people" at a time when this dream was far from being realized. Woodrow Wilson composed the "Fourteen Points" and challenged the United States to create a "world safe for democracy" at a time when emperors and kings ruled more than 80 percent of the world. Franklin Roosevelt's "Four Freedoms" raised the hopes and hearts of men.

These ideas, these dreams, gave us world leadership, not because we gave away money, but because we had ideas and ideals to offer.

Let us look at some of our present ideas to see if we should improve, modify, or even eliminate some of them in our dream government of the future.

The idea that "Politics is a dirty business" is the first one I nominate for oblivion. No one claims that banking is a dirty business because bank employees abscond with several million dollars each year. No one claims that the business profession is dirty and undignified because some businessmen try to bribe government officials. Nor does anyone claim that the legal profession is a dirty business because some lawyers are disbarred and some others consort with criminal elements. For we must look beyond the profession to discover the man who practices the profession, whether he is a politician or professor. And when we look into the political profession, we discover that actually all of us are the participants in an unending political drama.

It is the politician's task to translate the abstract, theoretical idea of the "common good" into concrete, working terms. The politician must decide how many dollars and cents constitute a "fair or just" minimum wage; whether public housing is required for the common good and, if so, how much; what to do about juvenile delinquency; whether to enter into trade relations and treaties with foreign governments. These political decisions control and create the very environment and atmosphere in which we live. And since the future always presents new problems, society can meet the future only with new answers—political answers.

Politics has been called the science by which man tries to create and maintain order in human affairs. But it is not a science like physics, based on the "laws" of the material universe. Politics deals with human beings, whose glory is their independence of mechanistic laws, whose welfare can be achieved only through agreement based on give and take, mutual respect and persuasion. Thus it is well said that "The man who is too good for politics is too good for his fellow man."

The second idea I nominate for oblivion is the idea that "The best government is the least government."

I was in Austria in 1936 when that country had very little government. The Chancellor of Austria, Engelbert Dollfuss, was assassinated, and for twenty-four hours there was no government at all. Gangs of marauders roamed the streets during the night, showing us what is to be expected when a country "enjoys," so to speak, the least government. Guatemala has had very little government. And they have a revolution, instead of an election, almost every four years!

Today business is complex and centralized; so is government. Sears, Roebuck and General Motors are examples of great growth, size, and improvement over their predecessors—two huge and successful corporations which are today three, four, and maybe five times as big as they were twenty-five years ago. When business grows at such speed and reaches such complexity, should we be surprised at the growth of government? The same is true of the labor movement. When labor and business have both grown so large, can we still maintain that the best government is the least government?

This phrase, "The best government is the least government," arose in the seventeenth century when all government was the tool of absolute royalty. Government was not a "service institution" then, as it is today. It was a money-making enterprise, designed to fill the pocketbooks of royalty and nobility. Habeas corpus was unknown or unrecognized; spies, stool pigeons, and snoopers invaded the private lives of the people; and more than 120 offenses in England—considered an advanced country at that time—were punishable by death. With government the exclusive domain of kings and princes who ran affairs to suit themselves, small wonder that the middle class claimed that the best government of that type was the least government.

The third idea, which I certainly do not wish to consign to oblivion but which is interesting to think about, is that profound statement in our Declaration of Independence: "All men are created equal."

When he wrote that clause, Jefferson meant, I believe, that all men are created equal before the law and equal in respect to their nature as human beings—spiritually equal. Jefferson did not mean that all men are created equal in all respects. For example, he believed that ownership of some property was necessary to qualify for voting privileges. He supported the early theory of our government that appointment to the U.S. Senate should be restricted to property owners and "elder statesmen."

Democracy calls upon us to promote equal opportunity and equal justice, but it is a false democracy which seeks to level all persons, and reduce to least common denominators all beliefs, all differences, and all values. You who are privileged persons cannot be content to achieve no more than the average. Everyone here is called to the heights of achievement—achievements which will be unreachable by those who frustrate themselves and society by attributing their problems to other people or to other countries.

And that is the fourth idea for reconsideration: the idea that foreigners and foreign wars are the cause of our troubles.

In our dream government of the future, let us stop blaming

others. We do this when we speak and act as if we believed that everything would be perfect if we could eliminate the Communist menace, or the tension between the Arabs and Jews, or overpopulation in Japan or India, or the ingratitude of nations which have received our foreign aid.

No war is a foreign war once we are in it. No problem is a foreign problem once it affects the lives of our people and the tranquillity of our society.

The young leaders of the YMCA have the chance to prepare now for the new government of the new world of the twenty-first century, now only some forty years away. Air transportation alone has revolutionized our concepts of geography and of national security. The jet age is already here. The rocket age is about to arrive. The farm has given way to the city, and local government designed in the eighteenth century for a rural nation must be changed to suit the huge metropolitan centers of the twentieth century. In the last five years our urban population has increased by almost twelve million. Our municipal and suburban governmental structures are out of date like a Model T Ford. They need remodeling by politicians and politically-conscious citizens devoted to the common good, knowledgeable in the art of good government, and perceptive enough to concentrate on the needs of the next generation. Let us modernize our whole government as we modernize our businesses and our medical and scientific practices, making it more responsive to all our needs.

5. An America of the Heart

Speaking at Providence College commencement exercises on June 2, 1964, Sargent Shriver called upon the new graduates to become not honorary but practicing doctors of humanities.

WHAT IS AMERICA NOW? It is an America of the plains and the seas. It has always been that. And now it is also an America of the blast furnace, of the oil wells and the great cattle ranches, of the huge dams and the hydroelectric power projects, of the high standard of living, of the Polaris submarines and the nuclear aircraft carriers, of the nineteen-story rockets and the sixty-story temples of finance. But it is also an America of concern for the aged and the disenfranchised, an America of the Peace Corps and the War on Poverty. It is an America that is beginning to shake off the despair and cynicism born out of the cold war, and to think and act again as if there were hope for the world. It is an America as it was when it started: a land of ideas and ideals.

Father Henri Pire, the Dominican priest who won the Nobel Prize in 1958, had an idea. He had many ideas and ideals. After World War II he started an organization called Aid to Displaced Persons that helped resettle homeless and uprooted victims of the war. He also founded a home for aged refugees, and helped these old people find jobs to sustain themselves. He organized the so-called European Villages, where displaced persons could settle and raise their families. And he launched a kind of crusade to awaken public opinion in the European nations about the plight of the displaced persons. He called this crusade, "A Europe of the Heart." Through it he tried to interest all Europe in the work of resettling refugees, and in the general idea of service to all persons in need.

Last December Father Pire visited Seton Hall University and told the students: "We must, before all, create a public opinion, objective and constructive, expressing clearly the will to live in a world free of racism, hunger, and war."

This is the kind of crusade I would like to enlist all of you in. Today I was presented an honorary degree as Doctor of Humanities. I would like all of you, whatever degree you have received, to be practicing doctors of humanity. I want you to join in creating an America of the Heart, an America free of racism, hunger, and despair.

We have let ourselves fall into the notion that these things can be done from the top of society, that government or business or science can improve the human condition by hiring enough administrators, or stepping up the production of autos, or developing new vaccines. But *real* changes, real improvements have to come from the depths of society, from the confrontation of persons. This is something we have learned in the Peace Corps.

Today our Volunteers are having a confrontation with persons in many other countries. Through them the world is discovering an America of the Heart, the America of ideas and ideals. The world is discovering the secret of America's greatness. And now we must put that secret to work in America itself.

This is the chance we have in President Johnson's proposed

War on Poverty. This program is aimed at wiping out the whole subculture of poverty in America.

You are not poor or you would not be here today, equipped with a splendid education. Yet there are twenty-five to thirty million poor—shut out, broken, and demoralized. We haven't even seen them, we are so enclosed in our middle-class life. They have had no spokesmen, no lobby.

The poor are the hardest people in our society to reach. It is like going down in a diving bell. The farther you get down into this alienated subculture, the harder and harder it is to penetrate another foot. But we must bring the poor back into our society.

In the Peace Corps we asked people to volunteer for work all over the world, not for money or glory, not even for comfort and convenience, but only to help others who needed and wanted their help. The same challenge exists in the United States in the War on Poverty at home. We will have Volunteers in Service to America—our own grass-roots "Peace Corps"—to work in state, local, or nonprofit programs to wipe out causes of poverty; to work with all the poor and the forgotten—perhaps right here in Providence.

Helping others is not a new idea. It is very old, as old as the Old Testament. It was old when St. Thomas wrote in the thirteenth century: "So powerful was the appeal of man's needs and so eloquent was the cry of man in his distress, in his poverty, in his sin, in his helplessness, that God heard this and was unable to resist it to the point that he sent his only Begotten Son to come into the world to seek and to save that which we lost."

Is the appeal of man's needs any less powerful today? Is his cry of distress, of poverty, of helplessness less eloquent? Can any of us resist it?

Someone wrote once that the old man wants peace and quiet, the middle-aged man wants love and respect, but the young man wants challenges. Well, you are two things above all today: You are bachelors of arts and you are young. So I leave you with these challenges: the challenge of St. Thomas, the challenge of Father Pire, the challenge of the Peace Corps, and the challenge of the War Against Poverty. . . . The challenge to heed an eloquent cry—the most eloquent cry of all—the cry of human beings in distress, here in America and across the world.

6. The Pietà of Michelangelo

Michelangelo's Pietà had been transported from Italy with infinite care to serve as the central attraction of the Vatican Pavilion at the New York World's Fair. This talk was prepared for the ceremony dedicating the Vatican Pavilion on April 19, 1964.

OUR CENTURY may be remembered in history by any one of several names, some ominous and some hopeful. But whatever the name, ours is certainly a century in which the nations have begun to speak to each other and to try to understand each other with an intensity of purpose and a sense of urgency unmatched in history.

It is also the century in which the various cultures of mankind try to speak to each other and learn from each other. And on the highest plane of human effort, in the realm of faith and in the silence of prayer, it is, more than any century we have known, an age in which men of all creeds are making the effort of mind and heart to understand their differences and find their common ground. It was this dialogue to which John XXIII dedicated the Vatican Council, and it is this dialogue which Paul VI already has intensified—through the continuation of the Vatican Council, through the subtle but eloquent modern fashions of liturgy (so that in a new sense it speaks in many tongues), through his pilgrimage to the East, and through such silent testimonies as this Vatican Pavilion.

A remarkable aspect of this occasion is the exhibit that stands at the head of this pavilion: the Pietà of Michelangelo.

To achieve the peace that goes beyond treaties, that goes beyond ideologies, a peace that binds hearts and creates a true community, we need the world of art to lift our spirits, and we need the world of religion to give us a better standard than the things we see around us. Here is that standard, in the sorrowing mother, holding what was failure as the world goes, but which proved to be the greatest triumph of all time.

It was triumphant because, as Michelangelo's Pietà reveals, it was a life of compassion. This is what we need to see and what we need to understand if the world is ever to know true peace. For the saints and sages of the great religions have always agreed that a peace that passes understanding can be reached only by compassion.

This is the ideal that must illumine, from the very center, all our efforts to bring a better life to our world, within our own country, and in the farthest reaches of the planet.

Just as this masterpiece has crossed the Atlantic unmarred, no ocean can be wide enough to exclude the compassion of Michelangelo's Pietà. And it is only with this compassion that man can look upon man—through the mask of many colors, through the vestments of many religions, through the dust of poverty, or through the disfigurement of disease—and recognize his brother.

7. In Spite of Everything

The 26th Annual Mass Conference of the United Jewish Appeal of Greater New York, held on April 19, 1964, honored the six million European Jews who were murdered by Nazi Germany. Shriver recalled the words of young Anne Frank, martyred at fifteen.

WE ARE HERE TO COMMEMORATE DEATH and to advance life.

It is difficult for the human mind to comprehend death, any death, the death of one human being we know and love. A senseless, needless death, a murder, is almost beyond comprehension.

We have just suffered such a loss in the American family. The whole world seems to have been moved by the death of John Kennedy.

But what can we say of the murder of six million Jews?

What can we say of the loss of one Anne Frank?

She has said all that can be said.

"It's really a wonder that I haven't dropped all my ideals," Anne Frank said before her death. "Yet I keep them, because in spite of everything I still believe that people are really good at heart."

In spite of everything, she was able to say that.

"I see the world gradually being turned into a wilderness," she wrote in her diary a month before she was taken. "I hear the ever approaching thunder, which will destroy us, too. I can feel the sufferings of millions and yet, if I look up into the heavens, I think it will all come right. In the meantime, I must uphold my ideals, for perhaps the time will come when I shall be able to carry them out."

Those are words that helped me in days like last November, that helped me understand what I saw last January in Jerusalem and in Galilee as I visited the living memorial to Anne Frank; they are words that can help us now. Let us look up into the heavens to keep our vision, but let us also keep working in the world. For the time has come when we *are* able to carry out those ideals.

You are doing just that. For twenty-six years, you have been doing it. You have accepted the terrible lessons of the 1930's and the 1940's, the lessons of dictators and war. You know that these tragedies rise out of earlier failures, out of conditions that should not have been permitted to exist, out of poverty and discrimination. You bear witness, as John Kennedy said of the birth of the State of Israel, "to humanity betrayed, 'plundered, profaned, and disinherited.'"

The lesson for us is to put an end to poverty, to discrimination, to the betrayal of human dignity.

Standing before the Lincoln Memorial on Lincoln's birthday, President Johnson stated our duty today. "The American promise will be unfulfilled, Lincoln's work—our work—will be unfinished," he said, "so long as there is a child without a school, a school without a teacher, a man without a job, a family without a home; so long as there are sick Americans without medical care or aging Americans without hope; so long as there are any Americans, of any race or color, who are denied their full human rights; so long as there are any Americans, of any place or region, who are denied their human dignity."

If we keep on with this work, if you continue to do your part, if state and local and national governments do their part, if together we keep this vision, then the wildernesses of the world can become a garden—a garden from which no one will be expelled, in which no one will be hungry, in which people can find peace.

Appendix A

PEACE CORPS NATIONAL ADVISORY
COUNCIL MEMBERS, 1961–1964

LYNDON B. JOHNSON, *Chairman*
WILLIAM O. DOUGLAS

Leona Baumgartner
Joseph Beirne
Harry Belafonte
Mrs. Janet Leigh Brandt
Mary I. Bunting
Rev. William Sloan Coffin
LeRoy Collins
Millard Cope
Rev. John J. Considine, M.M.
Colonel Henry Crown
Alfred Dent
Donald K. Emmerson
John H. Fischer
Arthur S. Flemming
J. Peter Grace
Mrs. Albert M. Greenfield
George H. Gibben
C. J. Haggerty

Fred Heinkel
Mrs. Oveta Culp Hobby
E. Palmer Hoyt
Roger W. Jones
Rabbi Benjamin M. Kahn
Mrs. Robert Kintner
Ralph Lazarus
David E. Lilienthal
Murray D. Lincoln
James A. McCain
John Macy
Frederic R. Mann
Benjamin Mays
Franklin Murphy
Mrs. E. Lee Ozbirn
Donald A. Petrie
Clarence E. Pickett
Roger Revelle

Rev. James H. Robinson

John D. Rockefeller IV

Eleanor Roosevelt

Eugene V. Rostow

George I. Sanchez

Mrs. Harvey B. Schechter

James Scott

Thomas J. Watson, Jr.

Benjamin C. Willis

Appendix B

UNITED STATES REPRESENTATIVES IN THE 46 NATIONS
SERVED BY THE PEACE CORPS,
1961–1964

Countries Served	Peace Corps Representatives		Number of Volunteers Who Have Served (Including Those Now in Training)
Cameroon	Chester C. Carter	1962–63	150
	Lawrence Williams	1963–	
Ethiopia	Harris Wofford	1962–64	734
	H. Donald Wilson	1964–	
Gabon	William N. Wilkes	1963–	98
Ghana	George E. Carter, Jr.	1961–64	254
	Francis L. Broderick	1964–	
Guinea	Henry R. Norman	1963–	69
Ivory Coast	Clyde B. MacKenzie	1962–63	109
	Robert J. MacAlister	1963–	
Liberia	Thomas H. Quimby	1962–64	454
	William H. Watson	1964–	
Malawi	Robert K. Poole	1962–64	277
	James E. Blackwell	1964–	
Niger	George J. Klein (Acting)	1963–64	59
	C. Payne Lucas	1964–	
Nigeria	Samuel D. Proctor	1961–63	835
	William G. Saltonstall	1963–	
Senegal	Hyman U. Hoffman	1962–	109
Sierra Leone	Walter C. Carrington	1961–63	287
	Donovan V. McClure	1963–	
Somali	Bert J. DeLotto	1962–63	108
	Salvatore P. Tedesco	1963–64	
	Frederick C. Thomas	1964–	
Tanganyika	Robert E. Hellawell	1961–63	356
	Martin N. Chamberlain	1963–	

Countries Served	Peace Corps Representatives		Number of Volunteers Who Have Served (Including Those Now in Training)
Togo	Robert Haves	1962–63	98
	Leonard Pompa	1963	
Indonesia	David S. Burgess	1963–64	51
	Derek S. Singer	1964–	
Malaysia	J. Norman Parmer	1961–63	604
	Lewis H. Butler	1963–64	
	James W. Gould	1964–	
Sabah/Sarawak	John Landgraf	1962–63	
	Joseph Fox	1963–64	
Philippines	Lawrence H. Fuchs	1961–63	1,014
	Bascom H. Story	1963–64	
	Maurice D. Bean	1964–	
Thailand	Glenn W. Ferguson	1961–63	433
	John C. McCarthy	1963–	
Bolivia	Derek S. Singer	1962–64	400
	Jasin Edwards	1964–	
Brazil	George M. Coleman	1962–64	767
	Warren G. Fuller	1964–	
British Honduras	David H. Stauffer	1962–64	59
	Richard F. Ware	1964–	
Chile	Marshall Nason	1961–62	435
	Rafael Sancho-Bonet	1962–64	
	William E. Moffett	1964–	
Colombia	Christopher B. Sheldon	1961–	985
Costa Rica	Francis H. Appleton	1963–	76
	Laurence P. Horan (Designate)		
Dominican Republic	Andres Hernandez	1962–64	266
	R. Lowell Satin	1964–	
Ecuador	Milton L. Carr	1962–63	537
	Eugene Baird	1963–	
El Salvador	Richard Hancock (Acting)		82
		May 1962–63	
	Richard Griscom (Acting)	1963–	
Guatemala	Ashby T. Harper	1962–64	167
	Andres Hernandez	1964–	

Countries Served	Peace Corps Representatives		Number of Volunteers Who Have Served (Including Those Now in Training)
Honduras	Tom Walz (Acting)	1962–63	161
	Edwin P. Astle	1963–	
	Joseph A. Farrell III (Designate)		
Jamaica	Jan W. Owen	1962–63	98
	Lester Spielman	1963–	
Panama	David J. Boubion	1963–	188
Peru	Frank F. Mankiewicz	1962–64	669
	Samuel Guarnaccia	1964–	
St. Lucia	Fred Brancel	1961–62	31
	William H. Watson	1963–	
Uruguay	Theodore P. Banks, Jr.	1963–	35
Venezuela	Roderic E. Buller	1962–63	393
	Milton L. Carr	1963–	
Afghanistan	Robert L. Steiner	1962–	144
Ceylon	Charles D. Moore (Acting)	1962–64	39
Cyprus	Meridan H. Bennett	1962–64	22
India	Roger Ernst (Acting)	1961–62	391
	Charles Houston	1962–	
Iran	William J. Cousins	1962–64	221
	Cleo F. Shook	1964–	
Morocco	Frederick C. Thomas	1962–64	224
	William T. Carter	1964–	
Nepal	Robert H. Bates	1962–63	192
	William Unsoeld	1963	
	William S. Warren	Jan.-May 1964	
	William Unsoeld	1964–	
Pakistan	F. Kingston Berlew	1962–64	353
	James H. Boughton	1964–	
Tunisia	Reuben Simmons (Acting)	1962–63	270
	Chester C. Carter	1963	
	Richard Graham	1963–	
Turkey	David Weinman (Acting)	1962–63	394
	Ross Pritchard	1963–	
			13,698

Index

235